CHEESECAKE
EXTRAORDINAIRE

CHEESECAKE
EXTRAORDINAIRE

*More than 100 Sumptuous
Recipes for the Ultimate Dessert*

MARY CROWNOVER

CB

CONTEMPORARY
BOOKS

CHICAGO

Library of Congress Cataloging-in-Publication Data

Crownover, Mary.
    Cheesecake extraordinaire / Mary Crownover.
       p.   cm.
    Includes index.
    ISBN 0-8092-3544-7 (pbk.)
    1. Cheesecake (Cookery)   I. Title.
TX773.C78   1994
641.8′653—dc20   94-12075
                                             CIP

Designed by Walter Gray Lamb

Photographed by Christopher Weeks
Photo credits follow index.

Contemporary Books paperback edition, 1994
Originally published by Taylor Publishing Company, Dallas, Texas, 1990

Published by Contemporary Books, Inc.
Two Prudential Plaza, Chicago, Illinois 60601-6790
Manufactured in the United States of America
International Standard Book Number: 0-8092-3544-7
10   9   8   7   6   5   4   3   2

To my husband, Dick,

my children, Richard, Hal, and Cathy,

my parents, Mary Frances and Burwell Humphrey, and

my sister, Jeanne Reece

I can vividly recall the day I met Mary on the way back to my office in the Nutrition Clinic. As we walked together, she talked excitedly about the cheesecake recipes she had been working so hard to perfect. She mentioned she had been bringing two cheesecakes a week the last year for people to taste and critique. She invited me to participate in the tasting and evaluation (a task I was most easily convinced to do, as I love cheesecake!). Still, I had to ask the question, since I had been teaching a great deal about weight control that day, how she remained so slender while making all those cheesecakes. She responded, as I hoped she would, that it was all in eating it in moderation and compensating for the extra calories by eating less in other places. It was so refreshing to hear this from someone besides myself for a change.

You see, I firmly believe that there is no such thing as a "fattening" food. No food is solely responsible for anyone being overweight. Obesity is a complex problem involving total caloric intake as well as total caloric output through activities and exercise. You can maintain a desirable weight through the proper combination of both of these; this combination can include cheesecake.

Does this balance apply to those concerned about saturated fats and heart disease? I believe it most certainly does. A diet which has a variety of fibers, controlled calories, and choices high in unsaturated fats or oils will tolerate cheesecake occasionally.

With these things in mind, I hope you will enjoy the recipes in *Cheesecake Extraordinaire*. As a cook, I admire the work and dedication Mary has put into bringing you her cheesecake recipes. As someone with a modestly refined palate, I guarantee you the cheesecakes I tasted were fabulous. And as a dietitian/nutritionist, I urge you to enjoy these recipes as part of an overall healthy eating and exercise program.

Rusty Foltz, R.D.
Cardiopulmonary Dietitian
Hammons Heart Institute
Springfield, Missouri

Special thanks are due to the many people who encouraged and supported me in the creation of these recipes. Their enthusiasm was overwhelming.

I want to thank Mary Kelly, my editor, with whom it has been a joy to work.

Thank you, Linda Woodrum, for the many hours of work you put into making this a more versatile cookbook.

I want to acknowledge Christopher Weeks, an outstanding photographer; I'm glad he did the photography for my book.

Thank you, Barb Barman, for being the best friend anyone could have and for proofreading everything I write.

I am grateful to Debbie Hardin, who has rendered numerous opinions on flavor combinations.

A sincere thanks goes to Ann Darden Heether, my very close friend. She is both a wonderful cook and a great inspiration.

And finally, thanks to Rusty Foltz, R.D., for being my friend and offering to write the foreword for this book.

Success Every Time:
Ingredients, Equipment, and Helpful Hints

Count on these tips to help you make each of your cheese-cakes an outstanding success.

Ingredients

Cheese
The cheese is the most prominent ingredient in all cheese-cakes, so choose it with care. Your best choice is cream cheese because it has a lower water content than neufchatel (60%), cottage cheese (78%), or ricotta (72%). This, combined with its higher butterfat content, produces a creamier texture.

Chocolate
For the best results, use high quality chocolate in the recipes that call for chocolate. Semisweet chocolate is made of pure chocolate, cocoa butter, and sugar. You can buy it in the form of chocolate chips and 1-ounce squares.

Milk chocolate is made of pure chocolate, cocoa butter, sugar, and milk solids. It is the most popular eating chocolate and gives cheesecakes a light chocolate flavor. Look for it in the form of chocolate chips and bars.

German chocolate is a sweet cooking chocolate made of

pure chocolate, cocoa butter, and sugar. It is sweeter than semisweet chocolate and is sold in 4-ounce bars.

White chocolate is also known as confectioners' coating and refers to a chocolate-like product that has cocoa butter but no cocoa solids. It is sold in the form of chips, bars, and blocks.

Cream
Whipping cream, also known as heavy cream, is used mainly as a cheesecake topping and sometimes in the fillings. For best results when whipping cream, use a chilled bowl and beaters and whip until stiff peaks form (tips stand straight).

Eggs
All the recipes were tested using U.S. Grade A large eggs. When adding eggs to your cheesecake, avoid overbeating them to prevent cracks.

Sugar
Granulated sugar and brown sugar are used extensively throughout the book. When measuring brown sugar, be sure to pack it tightly in the measuring cup. Powdered sugar is also used in some recipes. It does not need to be sifted when used in small amounts.

Thickeners

Cornstarch and all-purpose flour are used throughout the book to help thicken the cheesecake filling. Cornstarch is used more often than flour because it gives the cheesecake a finer texture.

Appliances and Equipment

Blenders and Food Processors

Use these kitchen appliances to purée fruits and chop nuts and to crush cookies to make the crumb crusts. For best results, don't overload the blender or processor with food before blending.

Electric Mixers

A heavy-duty mixer is the best appliance for thoroughly combining cheesecake ingredients. If you don't have a heavy-duty mixer, you can use a hand-held mixer. Either way, be sure to scrape the bowl often with a spatula during mixing.

Ovens

It makes no difference whether you have a gas or an electric oven to bake your cheesecake. However, accurate baking temperature is essential. Use an oven thermometer to check the temperature of your oven. If your oven bakes too hot or too cool, you'll need to adjust the settings accordingly.

Springform Pans

Good quality springform pans are essential when baking cheesecake. The removable bottom and metal clasp which releases the sides of the pan make it easier to cut and serve the cheesecake. All of the cheesecakes in *Cheesecake Extraordinaire* were baked using a 9-inch springform pan.

Cheesecake Basics

If you want a cheesecake with a creamy consistency, have all of the ingredients at room temperature before starting. To bring cream cheese to room temperature quickly, warm it in a 200° oven for 10 minutes. Or, remove the foil and place it on a microwave-safe plate in your microwave oven. Micro-cook on 50% power (medium) for 2 to 3 minutes. You can bring eggs to room temperature by submerging them in a bowl of warm water for 5 to 10 minutes.

Many of the crusts used in this book are not baked. To make them more crisp, chill them, uncovered, in the refrigerator while you prepare the filling.

Many cheesecakes leak during baking. Avoid a messy oven by placing the springform pan on a non-shiny baking sheet before baking.

Your cheesecake is done when the center looks firm. If the surface of your cheesecake has a wet or shiny look in the center, leave it in the oven a little longer. Simply remove the cake from the oven and run a knife around the inside edge of the pan to prevent the cake from cracking while it firms up. Then turn the oven off and return the cake to the oven for an additional 30 minutes to 2 hours or till the center is firm.

Cool your cheesecake to room temperature and then refrigerate it overnight, uncovered and before adding the topping or garnishes. Storing it uncovered will prevent moisture from forming on the surface.

Cheesecakes often crack. But you can reduce the chances of your cake cracking with these simple precautions. Do not overbeat the batter when adding the eggs. Beating too long or at too high a speed will cause concentric cracks. Always beat eggs using the lowest speed of your electric mixer.

Do not bake your cheesecake at too high a temperature. You can easily check the accuracy of your oven with an oven thermometer.

Do not overbake you cheesecake. Overbaking can cause the "Grand Canyon" crack.

Cracking also occurs during the cooling process. As a cake cools, it begins to shrink. If the filling sticks to the side of the pan, it will crack in the center. To avoid this, run a knife around the edge of the cake to separate the cheesecake from the pan.

Oops! Your cheesecake cracked. But don't worry . . . repairing a cracked cheesecake is easy. After your cheesecake cools, you can smooth away cracks and flaws with a hot, wet, sharp knife. Simply dip the knife in hot water and make your repairs. When repairing chocolate cheesecakes, use a hot, dry knife because water can discolor chocolate. After dipping your knife in hot water, quickly dry it off and repair your chocolate cheesecake.

It is easier to slice a cheesecake before putting on the topping. Run a knife around the inside edge of the springform pan. Remove the pan rim and slice the cake with a thin, sharp, hot knife. You can heat the knife by holding it under hot water or by submerging it in a pitcher of hot water, repeating as often as necessary. Or use dental floss instead of a knife to slice the cake.

Many of the cheesecake toppings are cooked on the stove top in a small saucepan. You may cook them in less time by using your microwave oven. Place the ingredients in a microwave-safe bowl and micro-cook on 100% power (high), stirring frequently.

Plan ahead and make your cheesecake at least 1 day in advance to allow the flavors to ripen.

The richer the cheesecake, the better it freezes. All of the cakes in this book freeze beautifully. To freeze your cheesecake, prepare it according to the recipe directions, except omit the topping. Place it on a tray and freeze, uncovered, for 6 hours or till firm. Remove the cheesecake and wrap it in heavy-duty foil or place it in a large freezer bag. Seal, label, and freeze your cheesecake for several months. Thaw the uncovered cheesecake in the refrigerator overnight or at room temperature for 2 to 3 hours. Put any toppings on your cheesecake after it has thawed.

Great Garnishes

Toasting Nuts
Bring out the crunchy goodness of nuts by toasting them. Simply spread a single layer of nuts in a baking pan. Bake in a 350° oven for 8 to 10 minutes or till light brown, stirring occasionally.

To toast nuts in your microwave oven, place the nuts in an even layer on a glass pie plate. Micro-cook, uncovered, on 100% power (high) for 5 to 7 minutes, stirring every minute, until golden.

It's easy to have toasted nuts always on hand. Simply toast a large amount of nuts and store them in a covered container in your freezer for several months.

Melting Chocolate
When melting chocolate, make sure the equipment you use is completely dry. Any moisture that comes in contact with the chocolate may cause it to stiffen as it melts. For speedy melting, use chocolate chips, or chop squares of chocolate before melting.

The most convenient way to melt chocolate is in a heavy saucepan over low heat. Be sure to stir the chocolate constantly and remove it from the heat as soon as it melts.

The most fool-proof method for melting chocolate is in a double boiler. Place water in the bottom of the double boiler so that it comes to within $1/2$ inch of the upper pan. Place the double boiler over low heat and stir the chocolate till it melts. The water in the double boiler should not boil while the chocolate melts.

A handy way to melt chocolate chips is by using your microwave oven. Place the chips in a microwave-safe bowl or container and micro-cook them on 100% power (high) until chocolate almost melts. Remove from oven and stir till melted and smooth.

Grating Fresh Coconut
Fresh coconut is available year round, so take advantage of it by adding its fresh taste to your next cheesecake. When buying a fresh coconut, shake it to make sure there is milk inside. Next check the eyes to make sure they are not wet or moldy.

To prepare coconut for grating, pierce the three eyes with an ice pick or screwdriver. Drain off the liquid. Bake the coconut at 350° for 20 minutes. Use a hammer to break the coconut into large pieces. Remove the meat from the shell and grate it with a little water in a food processor or blender. Drain, pat dry, and use as directed in the recipes. One medium coconut contains about 3 cups grated coconut.

Garnishing Techniques
Chocolate curls: Use a bar of milk chocolate at room temperature. Carefully draw a vegetable peeler across the surface of the chocolate, making thin strips that curl. For smaller curls, use the narrow side of the chocolate. For larger curls, use the wide surface.

Grated chocolate: Rub a cool, firm piece of chocolate across the grates of a hand grater. Clean the surface of the grater occasionally to prevent clogging.

Shaved chocolate: Using short, quick strokes, scrape a vegetable peeler across the surface of a cool, firm piece of chocolate.

Citrus twists: Thinly slice lemons, limes, or oranges. Using a sharp knife, cut into the center of each slice. Twist the ends in opposite directions.

Piping whipped cream: Fold back the top of a pastry bag and spoon whipped cream into it. Unfold the top of the bag and twist closed. Gently squeeze the bag to release the whipped cream. The design is determined by the size and type of tip you use.

Modifying Your Recipes

The recipes in this book were developed using a 9-inch springform pan. If your springform pan is smaller or larger, use this handy chart for converting the recipe to fit your pan. Simply find your pan size on the chart and multiply all the ingredients in the recipe by the number that corresponds to your pan size. For example, if you are using an 8-inch springform pan, multiply the ingredients by 0.8.

Pan size:

12 inch	1.8
10 inch	1.2
9½ inch	1.1
9 inch	1.0
8½ inch	0.9
8 inch	0.8
7 inch	0.6
6 inch	0.4
4 inch	0.2

Creating Your Own Masterpieces

Inventing your own cheesecake flavors is fun and rewarding. It gives you the opportunity to enjoy and show off your own creativity. And it's easy when you follow these simple rules.

You can substitute a liquid for an equal amount of another liquid, such as 1 cup pineapple juice for 1 cup orange juice. Or, substitute a dry ingredient for an equal amount of another dry ingredient, such as ⅓ cup chopped almonds for ⅓ cup chopped walnuts.

You can substitute fruits, but try to interchange fruits that have similar water contents. For example, blackberries, blueberries, and raspberries can all be interchanged in a recipe. The same is true with strawberries and cherries, chopped apples and chopped pears, and puréed bananas and puréed pears.

When substituting chocolate, be sure to use the same measurement or weight that is called for in the recipe. If substituting German chocolate for semisweet chocolate, decrease the sugar by ¼ cup. When replacing German chocolate with semisweet chocolate, add ¼ cup sugar to the recipe. Semisweet and milk chocolate can be interchanged in equal amounts with no adjustments.

Dark brown, light brown, and granulated sugars can be substituted for one another in equal amounts.

Did You Know . . .

The Greeks enjoyed a form of cheesecake nearly 3000 years ago and considered this luscious dessert a delicacy as well as a food fit for athletes competing in the Olympic games.

The Birth of Cream Cheese

In the late nineteenth century, two New York dairy farmers developed a rich, cream-based cheese, perhaps inspired by neufchatel cheese from France. This new high-fat cheese was developed for the Empire Cheese Company and eventually became known as Philadelphia Brand Cream Cheese.

Beverage-Based Cheesecakes

Grasshopper Cheesecake

This minty dessert tastes as good as the thick frosty after-dinner drink that goes by the same name.

Chocolate Mint Cookie Crust

11	chocolate mint or chocolate sandwich cream cookies, crushed
3 tablespoons	butter or margarine

In a small bowl stir together crushed cookies and melted butter or margarine till well combined. Press crumb mixture evenly onto the bottom of a greased 9-inch springform pan.

Crème de Menthe Filling

24 ounces	cream cheese
3/4 cup	sugar
5 teaspoons	cornstarch
3	eggs
1	egg yolk
2/3 cup	green crème de menthe liqueur
1 1/4 teaspoons	vanilla extract
3	chocolate mint sandwich cream cookies, coarsely crushed

In a large bowl combine cream cheese, sugar, and cornstarch. Beat with an electric mixer till smooth. Add eggs and egg yolk, one at a time, beating well after each addition. Beat in crème de menthe and vanilla extract. Stir in crushed cookies. Pour the cream cheese mixture over the crust.

Bake at 350° for 10 minutes. Lower the temperature to 200° and bake for 1 hour and 10 minutes or till the center no longer looks wet or shiny. Remove the cake from the oven and run a knife around the inside edge of the pan. Chill, uncovered, overnight.

Chocolate Glaze

1/2 cup	semisweet chocolate chips
1 tablespoon	shortening
	Shaved white chocolate

In a small saucepan melt chocolate chips and shortening over low heat, stirring constantly. Spread warm chocolate mixture over cheesecake. Garnish with shaved white chocolate. Chill till serving time. Makes 12 to 18 slices.

Amaretto Cheesecake

For crunchy almonds with a distinctive nutty flavor, be sure to toast them before adding them to the crust and the filling.

Vanilla Almond Crust

11	vanilla sandwich cream cookies, crushed
3 tablespoons	chopped almonds, toasted
3 tablespoons	butter or margarine, melted

In a small bowl stir together crushed cookies and chopped almonds. Add melted butter or margarine and stir till well combined. Press crumb mixture evenly onto the bottom of a greased 9-inch springform pan.

Amaretto Filling

24 ounces	cream cheese
2/3 cup	sugar
5 teaspoons	cornstarch
3	eggs
1	egg yolk
1/4 cup	whipping cream
1/2 cup	amaretto
2 teaspoons	almond extract
1/3 cup	chopped almonds, toasted

In a large bowl combine cream cheese, sugar, and cornstarch. Beat with an electric mixer till smooth. Add eggs and egg yolk, one at a time, beating well after each addition. Stir in whipping cream, amaretto, and almond extract. Stir in almonds. Pour the cream cheese mixture over the crust.

Bake at 400° for 10 minutes. Lower the temperature to 200° and bake for 1 hour and 15 minutes or till the center no longer looks wet or shiny. Remove the cake from the oven and run a knife around the inside edge of the pan. Turn the oven off; return the cake to the oven for an additional 30 minutes. Chill, uncovered, overnight.

Chocolate Amaretto Sauce

1/2 cup	semisweet chocolate chips
1 tablespoon	amaretto

In a small saucepan melt chocolate over low heat, stirring constantly. Add amaretto and stir till smooth. Drizzle chocolate mixture over cheesecake. Chill till serving time. Makes 12 to 18 slices.

Amaretto Chocolate Cheesecake

Impress your friends by serving this rich cheesecake at the next dinner party.

Chocolate Cookie Crust

11	milk chocolate sandwich cream cookies, crushed
3 tablespoons	butter or margarine, melted

In a small bowl stir together crushed cookies and melted butter or margarine till well combined. Press crumb mixture evenly onto the bottom of a greased 9-inch springform pan.

Amaretto Chocolate Filling

24 ounces	cream cheese
2/3 cup	sugar
1/4 cup	sour cream
5 teaspoons	cornstarch
3	eggs
1	egg yolk
1 teaspoon	vanilla extract
4 teaspoons	unsweetened cocoa powder
3 tablespoons	sugar
1/2 cup	amaretto
1/3 cup	chopped almonds, toasted
2 teaspoons	almond extract

In a large bowl combine cream cheese, 2/3 cup sugar, sour cream, and cornstarch. Beat with an electric mixer till smooth. Add eggs and egg yolk, one at a time, beating well after each addition. Beat in vanilla extract.

Remove 3/4 cup of the mixture and put into a small bowl; stir in cocoa powder and 3 tablespoons sugar. Set aside. Stir amaretto, chopped almonds, and almond extract into the remaining cream cheese mixture.

Pour half of the amaretto mixture over the crust. Spoon 2/3 cup of the cocoa mixture over the amaretto mixture. Pour the remaining amaretto mixture over the cocoa mixture. Top with remaining cocoa mixture. Without disturbing the crust, swirl the blade of a knife through the cake to create a marbling effect.

Bake at 425° for 10 minutes. Lower the temperature to 225° and bake for 1 hour or till the center no longer looks wet or shiny. Remove the cake from the oven and run a knife around the inside edge of the pan. Chill, uncovered, overnight.

Chocolate Almond Topping

2 cups	semisweet chocolate chips
1 tablespoon	butter or margarine
24 to 36	whole almonds
1/2 cup	whipping cream
1 tablespoon	amaretto

In a small saucepan melt chocolate and butter or margarine over low heat, stirring constantly. Dip almonds in chocolate mixture. Arrange on a waxed-paper-lined baking sheet. Chill till chocolate hardens.

Meanwhile beat whipping cream and amaretto with an electric mixer till stiff peaks form. Pipe whipped cream mixture around the edge of the cheesecake. Garnish with chocolate-dipped almonds. Chill till serving time. Makes 12 to 18 slices.

Coffee 'n' Cream Cheesecake

You don't have to be a coffee drinker to enjoy this flavorful cheesecake.

Vanilla Coffee Crust

1/4 cup	butter or margarine
1 teaspoon	instant coffee
1 3/4 cups	finely crushed vanilla wafers
3 tablespoons	sugar
3 tablespoons	chopped almonds, toasted

In a small saucepan melt butter or margarine. Stir in instant coffee till dissolved. In a medium bowl stir together crushed vanilla wafers, sugar, and chopped almonds. Stir in butter mixture till well combined. Press the crumb mixture evenly onto the bottom of a greased 9-inch springform pan. Set aside.

Coffee Filling

24 ounces	cream cheese
3/4 cup	sugar
5 teaspoons	cornstarch
3	eggs
1	egg yolk
2 teaspoons	instant coffee
2 teaspoons	hot water
2 teaspoons	vanilla extract
1/2 cup	whipping cream

In a large bowl combine cream cheese, sugar, and cornstarch. Beat with an electric mixer till smooth. Add eggs and egg yolk, one at a time, beating well after each addition. Stir together instant coffee and hot water till dissolved. Add coffee mixture and vanilla extract to cream cheese mixture; beat till smooth. Stir in whipping cream. Pour the cream cheese mixture over the crust.

Bake at 350° for 15 minutes. Lower the temperature to 200° and bake for 1 hour and 10 minutes or till the center no longer looks wet or shiny. Remove the cake from the oven and run a knife around the inside edge of the pan. Turn the oven off; return the cake to the oven for an additional 30 minutes. Chill, uncovered, overnight.

Easy Coffee Bean Topping

1 cup	whipping cream
1 tablespoon	sugar
1 tablespoon	coffee-flavored liqueur
	Chocolate coffee beans

In a small bowl beat whipping cream, sugar, and coffee-flavored liqueur with an electric mixer till stiff peaks form. Pipe whipped cream mixture around the edge of the cheesecake. Garnish with chocolate coffee beans. Chill till serving time. Makes 12 to 18 slices.

Eggnog Cheesecake

If you want to leave the rum out of this holiday-flavored cheesecake, simply increase the whipping cream to 1/2 cup.

Chocolate Cookie Crust

11	chocolate sandwich cream cookies, crushed
1/8 teaspoon	ground nutmeg
3 tablespoons	butter or margarine, melted

In a small bowl stir together the crushed cookies and nutmeg. Add melted butter or margarine and stir till well combined. Press crumb mixture evenly onto the bottom of a greased 9-inch springform pan. Set aside.

Eggnog Filling

24 ounces	cream cheese
3/4 cup	sugar
5 teaspoons	cornstarch
4	eggs
1	egg yolk
1 1/2 teaspoons	ground nutmeg
1 1/4 teaspoons	vanilla extract
1/3 cup	whipping cream
1/4 cup	vanilla-flavored liqueur
2 tablespoons	light rum

In a large bowl combine cream cheese, sugar, and cornstarch. Beat with an electric mixer till smooth. Add eggs and egg yolk, one at a time, beating well after each addition. Beat in nutmeg and vanilla extract. Stir in whipping cream, liqueur, and light rum. Pour cream cheese mixture over crust.

Bake at 350° for 15 minutes. Lower the temperature to 200° and bake for 1 hour and 10 minutes or until the center no longer looks wet or shiny. Remove the cake from the oven and run a knife around the inside edge of the pan. Chill, uncovered, overnight.

Fuzzy Navel Cheesecake

This fun-to-serve cheesecake is flavored with orange juice and peach schnapps and topped with an orange marmalade glaze.

Homemade Cookie Crust

3/4 cup	flour
2 1/2 tablespoons	sugar
1	egg, lightly beaten
1/4 cup	butter or margarine, softened
1/2 teaspoon	vanilla extract

In a medium bowl stir together flour and sugar. Add egg, butter or margarine, and vanilla extract. Beat with an electric mixer till well combined. With generously greased fingers, press the dough evenly onto the bottom of a 9-inch springform pan.

Bake at 350° for 12 to 15 minutes or till lightly browned. Remove from oven and set aside.

Refrigerated Cookie Dough Crust: In place of Homemade Cookie Crust, use 8 ounces of refrigerated sugar cookie dough. Slice dough according to package directions. Arrange dough slices in pan, starting on the outside edge and working your way into the middle. Press dough evenly onto the bottom of the pan. Bake as directed above.

Peachy Orange Filling

24 ounces	cream cheese
3/4 cup	sugar
1/4 cup	sour cream
5 teaspoons	cornstarch
3	eggs
1	egg yolk
1/2 cup	frozen orange juice concentrate, thawed
1/4 cup	peach schnapps
2 teaspoons	lemon juice
1 1/4 teaspoons	vanilla extract

In a large bowl combine cream cheese, sugar, sour cream, and cornstarch. Beat with an electric mixer till smooth. Add eggs and egg yolk, one at a time, beating well after each addition. Beat in orange juice concentrate, peach schnapps, lemon juice, and vanilla extract. Pour the cream cheese mixture over the crust.

Bake at 350° for 15 minutes. Lower the temperature to 200° and bake for 1 hour and 10 minutes or till the center no longer looks wet or shiny. Remove the cake from the oven and run a knife around the inside edge of the pan. Chill, uncovered, overnight.

Orange Marmalade Glaze

2/3 cup	orange marmalade
3 tablespoons	peach schnapps
1 1/2 tablespoons	cornstarch
1 1/2 tablespoons	frozen orange juice concentrate, thawed
2 teaspoons	lemon juice

In a small saucepan stir together marmalade, schnapps, cornstarch, orange juice concentrate, and lemon juice. Cook and stir till thickened and bubbly. Cook and stir 2 minutes more. Pour over cheesecake. Chill till serving time. Makes 12 to 18 slices.

Daiquiri Cheesecake

Pucker up for this refreshing lime-flavored cheesecake.

Graham Cracker Crust

1¼ cups	graham cracker crumbs
3 tablespoons	sugar
¼ cup	butter or margarine, melted

In a small bowl stir together crumbs and sugar. Add melted butter or margarine. Stir till well combined. Press crumb mixture evenly onto the bottom of a greased 9-inch springform pan. Set aside.

Lime and Rum Filling

24 ounces	cream cheese
¾ cup	sugar
5 teaspoons	cornstarch
4	eggs
1	egg yolk
¼ cup	light rum
½ cup	frozen limeade concentrate, thawed
3 tablespoons	lime juice

In a large bowl combine cream cheese, sugar, and cornstarch. Beat with an electric mixer till smooth. Add eggs and egg yolk, one at a time, beating well after each addition. Beat in rum, limeade concentrate, and lime juice. Pour the cream cheese mixture over the crust.

Bake at 350° for 15 minutes. Lower the temperature to 200° and bake for 1 hour and 10 minutes or till the center no longer looks wet or shiny. Remove the cake from the oven and run a knife around the inside edge of the pan. Chill, uncovered, overnight.

Lime Glaze

½ cup	frozen limeade concentrate, thawed
4 teaspoons	cornstarch
4 teaspoons	sugar
1 tablespoon	light rum
2 teaspoons	lime juice
1 teaspoon	finely shredded lime peel

In a small saucepan stir together limeade concentrate, cornstarch, sugar, rum, and lime juice. Cook and stir till thickened and bubbly. Cook and stir 2 minutes more. Remove from heat. Stir in lime peel. Pour over cheesecake. Chill till serving time. Makes 12 to 18 slices.

Grande Passion Cheesecake

This tropical-tasting cheesecake gets its great flavor from La Grande Passion liqueur.

Toasted Coconut Crust

1¾ cups	flaked or freshly grated coconut
3 tablespoons	butter or margarine, melted

In a small bowl stir together coconut and melted butter or margarine. Press the coconut mixture evenly onto the bottom of a greased 9-inch springform pan. Bake at 350° for 12 to 15 minutes or until golden. Set aside.

La Grande Passion Filling

24 ounces	cream cheese
⅔ cup	sugar
5 teaspoons	cornstarch
3	eggs
1	egg yolk
½ cup	La Grande Passion liqueur
1 tablespoon	lime or lemon juice
1¼ teaspoons	vanilla extract
1 8-ounce can	crushed pineapple, drained

In a large bowl combine cream cheese, sugar, and cornstarch. Beat with an electric mixer till smooth. Add eggs and egg yolk, one at a time, beating well after each addition. Beat in liqueur, lime or lemon juice, and vanilla extract. Stir in pineapple. Pour the cream cheese mixture over the crust.

Bake at 350° for 15 minutes. Lower the temperature to 200° and bake for 1 hour and 10 minutes or till the center no longer looks wet or shiny. Remove the cake from the oven and run a knife around the inside edge of the pan. Chill, uncovered, overnight.

Tropical Fruit Glaze

½ cup	frozen tropical citrus beverage concentrate, thawed
2 tablespoons	La Grande Passion liqueur
2 teaspoons	lemon juice
2 teaspoons	cornstarch
1 medium	kiwifruit, peeled and sliced

In a small saucepan stir together tropical beverage concentrate, liqueur, lemon juice, and cornstarch. Cook and stir till thickened and bubbly. Cook and stir 2 minutes more. Pour over cheesecake. Garnish with kiwifruit. Chill till serving time. Makes 12 to 18 slices.

Marbled Grasshopper Cheesecake

Rich chocolate cheesecake is swirled through creamy crème de menthe cheesecake to create a sensational combination.

Chocolate Mint Cookie Crust

11	chocolate mint or chocolate sandwich cream cookies, crushed
3 tablespoons	butter or margarine

In a small bowl stir together crushed cookies and melted butter or margarine till well combined. Press crumb mixture evenly onto the bottom of a greased 9-inch springform pan.

Marbled Mint Filling

24 ounces	cream cheese
2/3 cup	sugar
1/4 cup	sour cream
5 teaspoons	cornstarch
3	eggs
1	egg yolk
1 teaspoon	vanilla extract
5 teaspoons	unsweetened cocoa powder
2 1/2 tablespoons	sugar
1/2 cup	green crème de menthe liqueur

In a large bowl combine cream cheese, 2/3 cup sugar, sour cream, and cornstarch. Beat with an electric mixer till smooth. Add eggs and egg yolk, one at a time, beating well after each addition. Beat in vanilla extract.

Remove 3/4 cup of the mixture and put into a small bowl; stir in cocoa powder and 2 1/2 tablespoons sugar. Set aside. Stir crème de menthe into the remaining cream cheese mixture.

Pour half of the crème de menthe mixture over the crust. Spoon 2/3 cup of the cocoa mixture over the crème de menthe mixture. Pour the remaining crème de menthe mixture over the cocoa mixture. Top with remaining cocoa mixture. Without disturbing the crust, swirl the blade of a knife through the cake to create a marbling effect.

Bake at 350° for 15 minutes. Lower the temperature to 200° and bake for 1 hour and 10 minutes or till the center no longer looks wet or shiny. Remove the cake from the oven and run a knife around the inside edge of the pan. Chill, uncovered, overnight.

Chocolate Sour Cream Topping

1/2 cup	semisweet chocolate chips
3 1/2 tablespoons	sour cream
4 teaspoons	crème de menthe liqueur
4 teaspoons	sugar

In a small saucepan melt chocolate over low heat, stirring constantly. Stir in sour cream, crème de menthe, and sugar. Spread the warm chocolate mixture over the cheesecake. Chill till serving time. Makes 12 to 18 slices.

Hawaiian Tropics Cheesecake

Toasted Coconut Crust

1 3/4 cups	flaked or freshly grated coconut
4 teaspoons	coarsely chopped almonds, toasted
3 tablespoons	butter or margarine, softened

In a small bowl stir together coconut and almonds. Add butter or margarine and stir till well combined. Press the coconut mixture evenly onto the bottom of a greased 9-inch springform pan. Bake at 350° for 12 to 15 minutes or until golden. Set aside.

Tropical Fruit Filling

24 ounces	cream cheese
2/3 cup	sugar
5 teaspoons	cornstarch
4	eggs
1	egg yolk
1/3 cup	frozen tropical fruit-flavored juice concentrate, thawed
1/3 cup	tropical fruit schnapps
2 teaspoons	vanilla extract
1 8-ounce can	crushed pineapple, drained
1/2 cup	flaked or freshly grated coconut

In a large bowl combine cream cheese, sugar, and cornstarch. Beat with an electric mixer till smooth. Add eggs and egg yolk, one at a time, beating well after each addition. Beat in fruit juice concentrate, schnapps, and vanilla extract. Stir in pineapple and coconut. Pour the cream cheese mixture over the crust.

Bake at 350° for 15 minutes. Lower the temperature to 225° and bake for 1 hour and 10 minutes or till the center no longer looks wet or shiny. Remove the cake from the oven and run a knife around the inside edge of the pan. Chill, uncovered, overnight.

Tropical Fruit Topping

	Sliced star fruit
	Sliced mango
	Sliced papaya
1 cup	orange marmalade, heated

Before serving, arrange fresh fruit over cheesecake. Drizzle with warm marmalade. Makes 12 to 18 slices.

Jamaican Banana Cheesecake

You'll discover fresh banana, rum, and crème de cacao in this island cheesecake.

Chocolate Cookie Crust

11	milk chocolate sandwich cream cookies, crushed
3 tablespoons	butter or margarine, melted

In a small bowl stir together crushed cookies and melted butter or margarine till well combined. Press crumb mixture evenly onto the bottom of a greased 9-inch springform pan.

Banana Rum Filling

24 ounces	cream cheese
3/4 cup	sugar
2/3 cup	puréed banana (about 1 1/2 small bananas)
5 teaspoons	cornstarch
3	eggs
1	egg yolk
3 tablespoons	banana schnapps
3 tablespoons	white crème de cacao
3 tablespoons	light rum
2 teaspoons	vanilla extract

In a large bowl combine cream cheese, sugar, puréed banana, and cornstarch. Beat with an electric mixer till smooth. Add eggs and egg yolk, one at a time, beating well after each addition. Beat in banana schnapps, crème de cacao, rum, and vanilla extract. Pour the cream cheese mixture over the crust.

Bake at 350° for 15 minutes. Lower the temperature to 225° and bake for 1 hour and 10 minutes or till the center no longer looks wet or shiny. Remove the cake from the oven and run a knife around the inside edge of the pan. Turn the oven off; return the cake to the oven for an additional 30 minutes. Chill, uncovered, overnight.

Fresh Fruit Topping

	Fresh fruit, sliced
	Chocolate ice cream topping

Arrange fresh fruit over cheesecake. Drizzle with chocolate topping. Chill till serving time. Makes 12 to 18 slices.

Chocolate Irish Cream Cheesecake

This luscious dessert is richer than the Irish Cream Cheesecake thanks to whipping cream and melted chocolate in the filling.

Chocolate Cookie Crust

11	milk chocolate sandwich cream cookies, crushed
3 tablespoons	butter or margarine, melted

In a small bowl stir together crushed cookies and melted butter or margarine till well combined. Press crumb mixture evenly onto the bottom of a greased 9-inch springform pan.

Chocolate Irish Cream Filling

18 ounces	cream cheese
2/3 cup	sugar
5	eggs
2/3 cup	whipping cream
3/4 cup	Irish cream liqueur
1 1/4 teaspoons	vanilla extract
2 teaspoons	hot water
1 1/4 teaspoons	instant coffee
1 12-ounce package	milk chocolate chips, melted
	Sifted powdered sugar

In a large bowl combine cream cheese and sugar. Beat with an electric mixer till smooth. Add eggs, one at a time, beating well after each addition. Beat in liqueur and vanilla extract. Stir together hot water and instant coffee. Stir into cream cheese mixture. Stir in melted chocolate. Pour the cream cheese mixture over the crust.

Bake at 350° for 15 minutes. Lower the temperature to 200° and bake for 1 hour and 10 minutes or till the center no longer looks wet or shiny. Remove the cake from the oven and run a knife around the inside edge of the pan. Turn the oven off; return the cake to the oven for an additional 2 hours. Chill, uncovered, overnight.

Place a decorative stencil over the top of the cheesecake. Sift powdered sugar over the stencil. Carefully remove stencil. Chill till serving time. Makes 12 to 18 slices.

Irish Cream Cheesecake

Yes, it's as sumptuous as it sounds!

Chocolate Cookie Crust

11	milk chocolate sandwich cream cookies, crushed
3 tablespoons	butter or margarine, melted

In a small bowl stir together crushed cookies and melted butter or margarine till well combined. Press crumb mixture evenly onto the bottom of a greased 9-inch springform pan.

Irish Cream Filling

24 ounces	cream cheese
3/4 cup	sugar
2 1/2 tablespoons	unsweetened cocoa powder
5 teaspoons	cornstarch
4	eggs
1	egg yolk
3/4 cup	Irish cream liqueur
1 teaspoon	vanilla extract
2 teaspoons	instant coffee
2 teaspoons	hot water

In a large bowl combine cream cheese, sugar, cocoa powder, and cornstarch. Beat with an electric mixer till smooth. Add eggs and egg yolk, one at a time, beating well after each addition. Beat in Irish cream liqueur and vanilla extract. Stir together instant coffee and hot water; stir into cream cheese mixture. Pour the cream cheese mixture over the crust.

Bake at 350° for 15 minutes. Lower the temperature to 200° and bake for 1 hour and 10 minutes or till the center no longer looks wet or shiny. Remove the cake from the oven and run a knife around the inside edge of the pan. Turn the oven off; return the cake to the oven for an additional 30 minutes. Chill, uncovered, overnight. Makes 12 to 18 slices.

Mocha Cheesecake

Chocolate and coffee is a classic combination that tastes great in this lavish cheesecake.

Mocha Crust

1 1/4 cups	crushed vanilla wafers
2 tablespoons	unsweetened cocoa powder
1 teaspoon	instant coffee
1/4 cup	butter or margarine, melted

In a small bowl stir together crumbs, cocoa powder, and coffee. Add melted butter or margarine. Stir till well combined. Press crumb mixture evenly onto the bottom of a greased 9-inch springform pan. Set aside.

Mocha Filling

24 ounces	cream cheese
1/3 cup	sugar
5 teaspoons	cornstarch
3	eggs
1	egg yolk
2/3 cup	whipping cream
1/3 cup	hot water
1 teaspoon	instant coffee
2 teaspoons	vanilla extract
1 cup	semisweet chocolate chips, melted

In a large bowl combine cream cheese, sugar, and cornstarch. Beat with an electric mixer till smooth. Add eggs and egg yolk, one at a time, beating well after each addition. Stir in whipping cream. Stir together hot water and coffee. Add coffee and vanilla extract to cream cheese mixture, stirring till well combined. Stir in melted chocolate. Pour the cream cheese mixture over the crust.

Bake at 350° for 15 minutes. Lower the temperature to 200° and bake for 1 hour and 10 minutes or till the center no longer looks wet or shiny. Remove the cake from the oven and run a knife around the inside edge of the pan. Turn the oven off; return the cake to the oven for an additional 1 hour. Chill, uncovered, overnight.

Mocha Glaze

1/2 cup	semisweet chocolate chips
1 tablespoon	shortening
1 teaspoon	instant coffee

In a small saucepan melt chocolate chips and shortening over low heat, stirring constantly. Stir in coffee till dissolved. Spread warm chocolate mixture over cheesecake. Chill till serving time. Makes 12 to 18 slices.

Mai Tai Cheesecake

You'll find the fruity flavors of a classic Mai Tai cocktail in this rich and creamy cheesecake.

Toasted Coconut Crust

1¾ cups	flaked or freshly grated coconut
3 tablespoons	butter or margarine, melted

In a small bowl stir together coconut and butter or margarine till well combined. Press the coconut mixture evenly onto the bottom of a greased 9-inch springform pan. Bake at 350° for 12 to 15 minutes or until golden. Set aside.

Mai Tai Filling

24 ounces	cream cheese
¾ cup	sugar
5 teaspoons	cornstarch
4	eggs
1	egg yolk
⅓ cup	frozen orange juice concentrate, thawed
¼ cup	grenadine syrup
¼ cup	orange-flavored liqueur
¼ cup	light rum
2 teaspoons	vanilla extract

In a large bowl combine cream cheese, sugar, and cornstarch. Beat with an electric mixer till smooth. Add eggs and egg yolk, one at a time, beating well after each addition. Beat in orange juice concentrate, grenadine syrup, liqueur, rum, and vanilla extract. Pour the cream cheese mixture over the crust.

Bake at 350° for 15 minutes. Lower the temperature to 200° and bake for 1 hour and 10 minutes or till the center no longer looks wet or shiny. Remove the cake from the oven and run a knife around the inside edge of the pan. Chill, uncovered, overnight.

Orange Glaze

½ cup	frozen orange juice concentrate, thawed
4 teaspoons	lime juice
4 teaspoons	grenadine syrup
1 tablespoon	cornstarch
1 tablespoon	orange-flavored liqueur
1 tablespoon	light rum
	Fresh fruit, sliced

In a small saucepan stir together orange juice concentrate, lime juice, grenadine syrup, and cornstarch. Cook and stir till thickened and bubbly. Cook and stir 2 minutes more. Stir in liqueur and rum. Pour over cheesecake. Garnish with fruit. Chill till serving time. Makes 12 to 18 slices.

Margarita Cheesecake

This tequila-flavored cheesecake tastes like the popular drink it's named after, minus the salt.

Homemade Cookie Crust

¾ cup	flour
2½ tablespoons	sugar
1	egg, lightly beaten
¼ cup	butter or margarine, softened
½ teaspoon	vanilla extract

In a medium bowl stir together flour and sugar. Add egg, butter or margarine, and vanilla extract. Beat with an electric mixer till well combined. With generously greased fingers, press the dough evenly onto the bottom of a greased 9-inch springform pan.

Bake at 350° for 12 to 15 minutes or till lightly browned. Remove from oven and set aside.

Refrigerated Cookie Dough Crust: In place of Homemade Cookie Crust, use 8 ounces of refrigerated sugar cookie dough. Slice dough according to package directions. Arrange dough slices in pan, starting on the outside edge and working your way into the middle. Press dough evenly onto the bottom of the pan. Bake as directed above.

Margarita Filling

24 ounces	cream cheese
¾ cup	sugar
5 teaspoons	cornstarch
4	eggs
1	egg yolk
⅓ cup	frozen limeade concentrate, thawed
¼ cup	orange-flavored liqueur
3 tablespoons	tequila

In a large bowl combine cream cheese, sugar, and cornstarch. Beat with an electric mixer till smooth. Add eggs and egg yolk, one at a time, beating well after each addition. Beat in limeade concentrate, liqueur, and tequila. Pour the cream cheese mixture over the crust.

Bake at 350° for 15 minutes. Lower the temperature to 200° and bake for 1 hour and 10 minutes or till the center no longer looks wet or shiny. Remove the cake from the oven and run a knife around the inside edge of the pan. Chill, uncovered, overnight.

Lime Glaze

½ cup	frozen limeade concentrate, thawed
1 tablespoon	cornstarch
1 tablespoon	orange-flavored liqueur
1 teaspoon	tequila
	Fresh lime wedges

In a small saucepan stir together limeade concentrate and cornstarch. Cook and stir till thickened and bubbly. Cook and stir 2 minutes more. Stir in liqueur and tequila. Pour over cheesecake. Garnish with lime. Chill till serving time. Makes 12 to 18 slices.

Neapolitan Cheesecake

This is a sophisticated combination of chocolate, vanilla, and strawberry cheesecake.

Chocolate Cookie Crust

11	milk chocolate sandwich cream cookies, crushed
3 tablespoons	butter or margarine, melted

In a small bowl stir together crushed cookies and melted butter or margarine till well combined. Press crumb mixture evenly onto the bottom of a greased 9-inch springform pan.

Neapolitan Filling

24 ounces	cream cheese
⅔ cup	sugar
¼ cup	whipping cream
5 teaspoons	cornstarch
4	large eggs
1	egg yolk
3½ tablespoons	strawberry schnapps
3 drops	red food coloring
3½ tablespoons	vanilla-flavored liqueur
1¼ teaspoons	vanilla extract
3½ tablespoons	crème de cacao
2 tablespoons	unsweetened cocoa powder
2½ tablespoons	sugar

In a large bowl combine cream cheese, ⅔ cup sugar, whipping cream, and cornstarch. Beat with an electric mixer till smooth. Add eggs and egg yolk, one at a time, beating well after each addition. Beat in vanilla extract.

Remove 1⅓ cups of the mixture and put into a small bowl; stir in strawberry schnapps and food coloring. Set aside. Remove another 1⅓ cups of the mixture and put into a small bowl: stir in vanilla liqueur and vanilla extract. Set aside. Stir crème de cacao, cocoa powder, and 2½ tablespoons sugar into the remaining cream cheese mixture.

Pour the chocolate mixture over the crust. Pour the strawberry mixture over the chocolate mixture. Pour the vanilla mixture over the strawberry mixture.

Bake at 350° for 15 minutes. Lower the temperature to 200° and bake for 1 hour and 10 minutes or till the center no longer looks wet or shiny. Remove the cake from the oven and run a knife around the inside edge of the pan. Turn the oven off; return the cake to the oven for an additional 1 hour. Chill, uncovered, overnight.

Neapolitan Topping

½ cup	whipping cream
1 tablespoon	sugar
12 to 18	chocolate-dipped strawberries

In a small bowl beat whipping cream and sugar with an electric mixer till stiff peaks form. Pipe whipped cream mixture around the edge of the cheesecake. Garnish with chocolate-dipped strawberries. Chill till serving time. Makes 12 to 18 slices.

Nutty Colada Cheesecake

For a fresher taste and crunchier texture, use fresh coconut and toasted almonds.

Toasted Coconut Crust

1¾ cups	flaked or freshly grated coconut
4 teaspoons	coarsely chopped almonds, toasted
3 tablespoons	butter or margarine, softened

In a small bowl stir together coconut and almonds. Add butter or margarine and stir till well combined. Press the coconut mixture evenly onto the bottom of a greased 9-inch springform pan. Bake at 350° for 12 to 15 minutes or until golden. Set aside.

Pineapple Coconut Filling

24 ounces	cream cheese
⅔ cup	sugar
5 teaspoons	cornstarch
3	eggs
1	egg yolk
1 8-ounce can	crushed pineapple, drained
½ cup	amaretto
¼ cup	cream of coconut
2 teaspoons	vanilla extract
1 teaspoon	almond extract
¼ cup	coarsely chopped almonds, toasted
1 cup	flaked or freshly grated coconut

In a large bowl combine cream cheese, sugar, and cornstarch. Beat with an electric mixer till smooth. Add eggs and egg yolk, one at a time, beating well after each addition. Beat in crushed pineapple, amaretto, cream of coconut, vanilla extract, and almond extract. Stir in almonds. Pour the cream cheese mixture over the crust. Sprinkle with coconut.

   Bake at 350° for 15 minutes. Lower the temperature to 225° and bake for 1 hour and 10 minutes or till the center no longer looks wet or shiny. Remove the cake from the oven and run a knife around the inside edge of the pan. Turn the oven off; return the cake to the oven for an additional 30 minutes. Chill, uncovered, overnight. Makes 12 to 18 slices.

Orange Pineapple Cheesecake

If you can't find frozen pineapple orange juice concentrate, use frozen orange juice concentrate and 1 teaspoon imitation pineapple extract instead.

Toasted Coconut Crust

1¾ cups	flaked or freshly grated coconut
4 teaspoons	coarsely chopped almonds, toasted
3 tablespoons	butter or margarine, softened

In a small bowl stir together coconut and almonds. Add butter or margarine and stir till well combined. Press the coconut mixture evenly onto the bottom of a greased 9-inch springform pan. Bake at 350° for 12 to 15 minutes or until golden. Set aside.

Orange Pineapple Filling

24 ounces	cream cheese
¾ cup	sugar
2 tablespoons	sour cream
5 teaspoons	cornstarch
3	eggs
1	egg yolk
⅓ cup	frozen pineapple orange juice concentrate, thawed
¼ cup	orange-flavored liqueur
2 tablespoons	light rum
2 teaspoons	vanilla extract

In a large bowl combine cream cheese, sugar, sour cream, and cornstarch. Beat with an electric mixer till smooth. Add eggs and egg yolk, one at a time, beating well after each addition. Beat in juice concentrate, liqueur, rum, and vanilla extract. Pour the cream cheese mixture over the crust.

   Bake at 350° for 15 minutes. Lower the temperature to 200° and bake for 1 hour and 10 minutes or till the center no longer looks wet or shiny. Remove the cake from the oven and run a knife around the inside edge of the pan. Chill, uncovered, overnight.

Orange Pineapple Glaze

¹/₃ cup	frozen orange pineapple concentrate, thawed
1 tablespoon	cornstarch
2 tablespoons	orange-flavored liqueur
2 tablespoons	flaked or freshly grated coconut

In a small saucepan stir together juice concentrate and cornstarch. Cook and stir till thickened and bubbly. Cook and stir 2 minutes more. Stir in liqueur. Remove from heat and stir in the coconut. Pour over cheesecake. Chill till serving time. Makes 12 to 18 slices.

Pina Colada Cheesecake

Make this refreshing cheesecake for the next pool party or beach bash.

Homemade Cookie Crust

1 cup	flour
3¹/₂ tablespoons	sugar
1	egg, lightly beaten
¹/₄ cup	butter or margarine, softened
¹/₂ teaspoon	vanilla extract

In a medium bowl stir together flour and sugar. Add egg, butter or margarine, and vanilla extract. Beat with an electric mixer till well combined. With generously greased fingers, press the dough evenly onto the bottom of a greased 9-inch springform pan.

Bake at 350° for 12 to 15 minutes or till lightly browned. Remove from oven and set aside.

Refrigerated Cookie Dough Crust: In place of Homemade Cookie Crust, use 8 ounces of refrigerated sugar cookie dough. Slice dough according to package directions. Arrange dough slices in pan, starting on the outside edge and working your way into the middle. Press dough evenly onto the bottom of the pan. Bake as directed above.

Pina Colada Filling

24 ounces	cream cheese
³/₄ cup	sugar
5 teaspoons	cornstarch
3	eggs
1	egg yolk
1 8-ounce can	crushed pineapple, drained
¹/₃ cup	grated coconut
¹/₄ cup	frozen pineapple juice concentrate, thawed
¹/₄ cup	cream of coconut
¹/₄ cup	light rum

In a large bowl combine cream cheese, sugar, and cornstarch. Beat with an electric mixer till smooth. Add eggs and egg yolk, one at a time, beating well after each addition. Stir in crushed pineapple, coconut, juice concentrate, cream of coconut, and rum. Pour the cream cheese mixture over the crust.

Bake at 350° for 15 minutes. Lower the temperature to 225° and bake for 1 hour and 10 minutes or till the center no longer looks wet or shiny. Remove the cake from the oven and run a knife around the inside edge of the pan. Turn the oven off; return the cake to the oven for an additional 1 hour. Chill, uncovered, overnight.

Easy Fruit Topping

1 cup	whipping cream
1 tablespoon	sugar
1 tablespoon	light rum
¹/₄ cup	grated coconut
	Fresh pineapple, sliced

In a small bowl beat whipping cream, sugar, and rum with an electric mixer till stiff peaks form. Fold in coconut. Pipe whipped cream mixture around the edge of the cheesecake. Garnish with fresh pineapple. Chill till serving time. Makes 12 to 18 slices.

Pink Lemonade Cheesecake

Lemon Cookie Crust

11	lemon sandwich cream cookies, crushed
3 tablespoons	butter or margarine, melted

In a small bowl stir together crushed cookies and melted butter or margarine till well combined. Press crumb mixture evenly onto the bottom of a greased 9-inch springform pan. Set aside.

Lemonade Filling

24 ounces	cream cheese
³/₄ cup	sugar
5 teaspoons	cornstarch
4	eggs
1	egg yolk
³/₄ cup	frozen pink lemonade concentrate, thawed
2 teaspoons	vanilla extract
2 drops	red food coloring (optional)

In a large bowl combine cream cheese, sugar, and cornstarch. Beat with an electric mixer till smooth. Add eggs and egg yolk, one at a time, beating well after each addition. Beat in lemonade concentrate, vanilla extract, and if desired, food coloring. Pour the cream cheese mixture over the crust.

Bake at 350° for 15 minutes. Lower the temperature to 200° and bake for 1 hour and 10 minutes or till the center no longer looks wet or shiny. Remove the cake from the oven and run a knife around the inside edge of the pan. Turn the oven off; return the cake to the oven for an additional 1 hour. Chill, uncovered, overnight.

Lemonade Glaze

¹/₃ cup	frozen pink lemonade concentrate, thawed
4 teaspoons	lemon juice
1 tablespoon	cornstarch
1 drop	red food coloring (optional)
	Lemon slices

In a small saucepan stir together lemonade concentrate, lemon juice, cornstarch, and if desired, food coloring. Cook and stir till thickened and bubbly. Cook and stir 2 minutes more. Pour over cheesecake. Garnish with lemon. Chill till serving time. Makes 12 to 18 slices.

Rum Raisin Cheesecake

This soothing cheesecake is like rum raisin ice cream except it holds a cut edge.

Vanilla Cookie Crust

11	vanilla sandwich cream cookies, crushed
¹/₄ cup	golden raisins
3 tablespoons	butter or margarine, melted

In a small bowl stir together crushed cookies and raisins. Stir in melted butter or margarine till well combined. Press crumb mixture evenly onto the bottom of a greased 9-inch springform pan.

Rum Raisin Filling

²/₃ cup	golden raisins
¹/₄ cup	light rum
24 ounces	cream cheese
²/₃ cup	sugar
¹/₄ cup	whipping cream
5 teaspoons	cornstarch
4	eggs
1	egg yolk
¹/₂ cup	vanilla-flavored liqueur
2 teaspoons	vanilla extract

Soak raisins in light rum for 1 hour. Drain, reserving rum. If necessary, add more rum to measure 2 tablespoons. In a large bowl combine cream cheese, sugar, and cornstarch. Beat with an electric mixer till smooth. Add eggs and egg yolk, one at a time, beating well after each addition. Stir in raisins, reserved rum, liqueur, and vanilla extract. Pour the cream cheese mixture over the crust.

Bake at 350° for 15 minutes. Lower the temperature to 225° and bake for 1 hour and 10 minutes or till the center no longer looks wet or shiny. Remove the cake from the oven and run a knife around the inside edge of the pan. Turn the oven off; return the cake to the oven for an additional 1 hour. Chill, uncovered, overnight.

Strawberry Daiquiri Cheesecake

Make this very berry dessert when fresh strawberries are in season.

Vanilla Cookie Crust

11	vanilla sandwich cream cookies, crushed
3 tablespoons	butter or margarine, melted

In a small bowl stir together crushed cookies and melted butter or margarine till well combined. Press crumb mixture evenly onto the bottom of a greased 9-inch springform pan.

Strawberry Filling

24 ounces	cream cheese
3/4 cup	sugar
5 teaspoons	cornstarch
3	eggs
1	egg yolk
1/4 cup	light rum
3 tablespoons	lime juice
3/4 cup	sliced strawberries

In a large bowl combine cream cheese, sugar, and cornstarch. Beat with an electric mixer till smooth. Add eggs and egg yolk, one at a time, beating well after each addition. Beat in rum and lime juice. Stir in sliced strawberries. Pour the cream cheese mixture over the crust.

Bake at 350° for 15 minutes. Lower the temperature to 225° and bake for 1 hour and 10 minutes or till the center no longer looks wet or shiny. Remove the cake from the oven and run a knife around the inside edge of the pan. Chill, uncovered, overnight.

Strawberry Glaze

2/3 cup	strawberry preserves
1 tablespoon	cornstarch
2 teaspoons	lemon or lime juice
1 tablespoon	light rum
	Whole strawberries

In a small saucepan stir together preserves, cornstarch, and lemon or lime juice. Cook and stir till thickened and bubbly. Cook and stir 2 minutes more. Stir in rum. Pour over cheesecake. Garnish with strawberries. Chill till serving time. Makes 12 to 18 slices.

Vandermint Cheesecake

Vandermint is a chocolate and mint-flavored liqueur. Look for it at your liquor store.

Chocolate Cookie Crust

11	chocolate mint sandwich cream cookies, crushed
3 tablespoons	butter or margarine, melted

In a small bowl stir together crushed cookies and melted butter or margarine till well combined. Press crumb mixture evenly onto the bottom of a greased 9-inch springform pan.

Vandermint Filling

24 ounces	cream cheese
3/4 cup	sugar
2 tablespoons	whipping cream
5 teaspoons	cornstarch
4	eggs
1	egg yolk
2/3 cup	Vandermint liqueur
1 teaspoon	vanilla extract

In a large bowl combine cream cheese, sugar, whipping cream, and cornstarch. Beat with an electric mixer till smooth. Add eggs and egg yolk, one at a time, beating well after each addition. Beat in liqueur and vanilla extract. Pour the cream cheese mixture over the crust.

Bake at 350° for 15 minutes. Lower the temperature to 200° and bake for 1 hour and 10 minutes or till the center no longer looks wet or shiny. Remove the cake from the oven and run a knife around the inside edge of the pan. Chill, uncovered, overnight.

Easy Mint Topping

1 cup	whipping cream
1 tablespoon	sugar
1 tablespoon	Vandermint liqueur
	Chocolate-covered mints

In a small bowl beat whipping cream, sugar, and liqueur with an electric mixer till stiff peaks form. Pipe whipped cream mixture around the edge of the cheesecake. Garnish with mints. Chill till serving time. Makes 12 to 18 slices.

Candy and Cookie Cheesecakes

Chocolate Candy Cheesecake

Candy-coated milk chocolate pieces are the candy of choice in this colorful cheesecake.

Chocolate Cookie and Candy Crust

11	milk chocolate sandwich cream cookies, crushed
¼ cup	candy-coated milk chocolate pieces, chopped
3 tablespoons	butter or margarine, melted

In a small bowl stir together crushed cookies and chopped candy. Stir in melted butter or margarine till well combined. Press crumb mixture evenly onto the bottom of a greased 9-inch springform pan.

Chocolate Candy Filling

24 ounces	cream cheese
⅓ cup	dark brown sugar
¼ cup	dark corn syrup
5 teaspoons	cornstarch
3	eggs
1	egg yolk
1 cup	milk chocolate chips, melted
⅓ cup	whipping cream
2 teaspoons	vanilla extract
1 cup	candy-coated milk chocolate pieces

In a large bowl combine cream cheese, brown sugar, corn syrup, and cornstarch. Beat with an electric mixer till smooth. Add eggs and egg yolk, one at a time, beating well after each addition. Stir in melted chocolate, whipping cream, and vanilla extract. Stir in chocolate pieces. Pour the cream cheese mixture over the crust.

Bake at 350° for 15 minutes. Lower the temperature to 200° and bake for 1 hour and 10 minutes or till the center no longer looks wet or shiny. Remove the cake from the oven and run a knife around the inside edge of the pan. Turn the oven off; return the cake to the oven for an additional 1 hour. Chill, uncovered, overnight.

Creamy Chocolate Topping

3 tablespoons	butter or margarine
2 cups	sifted powdered sugar
1/4 cup	unsweetened cocoa powder
1 teaspoon	vanilla extract
1 teaspoon	milk
	Candy-coated milk chocolate pieces

In a small mixing bowl beat butter or margarine till smooth. Gradually add 1 cup of the powdered sugar and cocoa powder, beating well. Slowly beat in vanilla and milk. Add remaining powdered sugar and beat till smooth. Add more milk, if necessary, for better spreading consistency. Spread chocolate mixture over cheesecake. Garnish with candy-coated milk chocolate pieces. Chill till serving time. Makes 12 to 18 slices.

Cookies and Cream Cheesecake

Choose your favorite brand of chocolate sandwich cream cookies to use in this filling cheesecake.

Chocolate Cookie Crust

11	milk chocolate sandwich cream cookies, crushed
3 tablespoons	butter or margarine, melted

In a small bowl stir together crushed cookies and melted butter or margarine till well combined. Press crumb mixture evenly onto the bottom of a greased 9-inch springform pan.

Creamy Cookie Filling

24 ounces	cream cheese
1/3 cup	sugar
5 teaspoons	cornstarch
3	eggs
1	egg yolk
2/3 cup	whipping cream
1/3 cup	dark crème de cacao
2 teaspoons	vanilla extract
1 cup	semisweet chocolate chips, melted
4	chocolate sandwich cream cookies, coarsely crumbled

In a large bowl combine cream cheese, sugar, and cornstarch. Beat with an electric mixer till smooth. Add eggs and egg yolk, one at a time, beating well after each addition. Stir in whipping cream, crème de cacao, and vanilla extract. Stir in melted chocolate. Fold in cookies. Pour the cream cheese mixture over the crust.

   Bake at 350° for 15 minutes. Lower the temperature to 200° and bake for 1 hour and 10 minutes or till the center no longer looks wet or shiny. Remove the cake from the oven and run a knife around the inside edge of the pan. Turn the oven off; return the cake to the oven for an additional 1 hour. Chill, uncovered, overnight.

Chocolate Cookie Topping

1 cup	whipping cream
1 tablespoon	sugar
4	chocolate sandwich cream cookies, coarsely crumbled

In a small bowl beat whipping cream and sugar with an electric mixer till stiff peaks form. Spread whipped cream mixture over cheesecake. Sprinkle with cookies. Chill till serving time. Makes 12 to 18 slices.

Butterscotch Cheesecake

Vanilla Cookie Crust

11	vanilla sandwich cream cookies, crushed
3 tablespoons	butter or margarine, melted

In a small bowl stir together crushed cookies and melted butter or margarine till well combined. Press crumb mixture evenly onto the bottom of a greased 9-inch springform pan.

Butterscotch Filling

24 ounces	cream cheese
¾ cup	dark brown sugar
5 teaspoons	cornstarch
3	eggs
1	egg yolk
½ cup	butterscotch schnapps
¼ cup	sour cream
2 teaspoons	vanilla extract

In a large bowl combine cream cheese, brown sugar, and cornstarch. Beat with an electric mixer till smooth. Add eggs and egg yolk, one at a time, beating well after each addition. Beat in butterscotch schnapps, sour cream, and vanilla extract. Pour the cream cheese mixture over the crust.

Bake at 350° for 15 minutes. Lower the temperature to 200° and bake for 1 hour and 10 minutes or till the center no longer looks wet or shiny. Remove the cake from the oven and run a knife around the inside edge of the pan. Turn the oven off; return the cake to the oven for an additional 1 hour. Chill, uncovered, overnight.

Butterscotch Whipped Cream Topping

1 cup	whipping cream
1 tablespoon	dark brown sugar
1 tablespoon	butterscotch schnapps
½ cup	coarsely crushed butterscotch candies

In a small bowl beat whipping cream, brown sugar, and schnapps with an electric mixer till stiff peaks form. Pipe whipped cream mixture around the edge of the cheesecake. Sprinkle with butterscotch candies. Chill till serving time. Makes 12 to 18 slices.

Butter Rum Cheesecake

To get the most rum flavor, be sure to use dark rum in the filling.

Vanilla Cookie Crust

11	vanilla sandwich cream cookies, crushed
3 tablespoons	butter or margarine, melted

In a small bowl stir together crushed cookies and melted butter or margarine till well combined. Press crumb mixture evenly onto the bottom of a greased 9-inch springform pan.

Butter Rum Filling

24 ounces	cream cheese
⅔ cup	dark brown sugar
¼ cup	dark corn syrup
6 tablespoons	butter or margarine, melted
¼ cup	whipping cream
5 teaspoons	cornstarch
4	eggs
1	egg yolk
1 tablespoon	dark rum
2 teaspoons	vanilla extract

In a large bowl combine cream cheese, brown sugar, corn syrup, butter or margarine, whipping cream, and cornstarch. Beat with an electric mixer till smooth. Add eggs and egg yolk, one at a time, beating well after each addition. Beat in rum and vanilla extract. Pour the cream cheese mixture over the crust.

Bake at 350° for 15 minutes. Lower the temperature to 200° and bake for 1 hour and 10 minutes or till the center no longer looks wet or shiny. Remove the cake from the oven and run a knife around the inside edge of the pan. Chill, uncovered, overnight. Makes 12 to 18 slices.

Turtle Cheesecake

Yep! This decadent cheesecake tastes just like the popular "turtle" candies.

Chocolate Cookie Crust

11	milk chocolate sandwich cream cookies, crushed
3 tablespoons	chopped pecans
3 tablespoons	butter or margarine, melted

In a small bowl stir together crushed cookies and pecans. Stir in melted butter or margarine till well combined. Press crumb mixture evenly onto the bottom of a greased 9-inch springform pan.

Chocolate Pecan Filling

24 ounces	cream cheese
$^2/_3$ cup	dark brown sugar
$^1/_3$ cup	dark corn syrup
5 teaspoons	cornstarch
3	eggs
1	egg yolk
1$^1/_4$ teaspoons	vanilla extract
5 teaspoons	unsweetened cocoa powder
2$^1/_2$ tablespoons	dark brown sugar
$^1/_2$ cup	praline-flavored liqueur
$^1/_4$ cup	chopped pecans

In a large bowl combine cream cheese, $^2/_3$ cup brown sugar, corn syrup, and cornstarch. Beat with an electric mixer till smooth. Add eggs and egg yolk, one at a time, beating well after each addition. Beat in vanilla extract.

Remove $^2/_3$ cup of the mixture and put into a small bowl; stir in cocoa powder and 2$^1/_2$ tablespoons brown sugar. Set aside. Stir liqueur and chopped pecans into the remaining cream cheese mixture.

Pour half of the pecan mixture over the crust. Spoon half of the cocoa mixture over the pecan mixture. Pour the remaining pecan mixture over the cocoa mixture. Top with remaining cocoa mixture. Without disturbing the crust, swirl the blade of a knife through the cake to create a marbling effect.

Bake at 325° for 15 minutes. Lower the temperature to 225° and bake for 1 hour or till the center no longer looks wet or shiny. Remove the cake from the oven and run a knife around the inside edge of the pan. Turn the oven off; return the cake to the oven for an additional 1 hour. Chill, uncovered, overnight.

Chocolate Pecan Topping

$^1/_2$ cup	milk chocolate chips
4 tablespoons	sour cream
	Pecan halves
6	individually wrapped vanilla caramels

In a small saucepan melt chocolate over low heat, stirring constantly. Stir in 3 tablespoons of the sour cream; spread over cheesecake. Arrange pecan halves over chocolate mixture. In the top of a double boiler melt caramels. Stir in remaining tablespoon of sour cream. Drizzle over chocolate and pecans. Chill till serving time. Makes 12 to 18 slices.

Praline Cheesecake

This cheesecake will remind you of the classic Southern candy.

Vanilla Pecan Cookie Crust

11	vanilla sandwich cream cookies, crushed
3 tablespoons	chopped pecans
3 tablespoons	butter or margarine, melted

In a small bowl stir together crushed cookies and pecans. Stir in melted butter or margarine till well combined. Press crumb mixture evenly onto the bottom of a greased 9-inch springform pan.

Praline Filling

24 ounces	cream cheese
2/3 cup	dark brown sugar
1/3 cup	dark corn syrup
5 teaspoons	cornstarch
3	eggs
1	egg yolk
1/2 cup	praline-flavored liqueur
2 teaspoons	vanilla extract
2/3 cup	chopped pecans

In a large bowl combine cream cheese, brown sugar, corn syrup, and cornstarch. Beat with an electric mixer till smooth. Add eggs and egg yolk, one at a time, beating well after each addition. Beat in liqueur and vanilla extract. Stir in pecans. Pour the cream cheese mixture over the crust.

Bake at 350° for 15 minutes. Lower the temperature to 200° and bake for 1 hour and 10 minutes or till the center no longer looks wet or shiny. Remove the cake from the oven and run a knife around the inside edge of the pan. Turn the oven off; return the cake to the oven for an additional 1 hour. Chill, uncovered, overnight.

Caramel Pecan Topping

1/2 cup	chopped pecans
11	individually wrapped vanilla caramels
2 tablespoons	sour cream

Sprinkle the pecans over the top of the cheesecake. In the top of a double boiler melt caramels. Stir in sour cream. Drizzle over pecans. Chill till serving time. Makes 12 to 18 slices.

Caramel Cheesecakes

Caramel Chocolate Chunk Cheesecake

This outstanding caramel cheesecake is topped with chunks of semisweet chocolate halfway through baking.

Nutty Oatmeal Crust

³/₄ cup	quick rolled oats
³/₄ cup	chopped walnuts or pecans
³/₄ cup	light brown sugar
¹/₂ teaspoon	ground cinnamon (optional)
¹/₄ cup	butter or margarine, melted

In a medium bowl stir together rolled oats, chopped nuts, brown sugar, and if desired, cinnamon. Add melted butter or margarine and stir till well combined. Press crumb mixture evenly onto the bottom of a greased 9-inch springform pan. Bake at 350° for 18 to 20 minutes or till light brown. Cool.

Caramel Filling

24 ounces	cream cheese
¹/₃ cup	dark brown sugar
¹/₃ cup	dark corn syrup
5 teaspoons	cornstarch
3	eggs
1	egg yolk
1 ¹/₂ teaspoons	vanilla extract
1 cup	chocolate chunks

In a large bowl combine cream cheese, brown sugar, corn syrup, and cornstarch. Beat with an electric mixer till smooth. Add eggs and egg yolk, one at a time, beating well after each addition. Stir in vanilla extract. Pour cream cheese mixture over the crust.

Bake at 350° for 15 minutes. Lower the temperature to 225° and bake for 40 minutes. Sprinkle the top with chocolate chunks. Return to the oven and bake about 35 minutes more or till the center no longer looks wet or shiny. Remove the cake from the oven and run a knife around the inside edge of the pan. Turn the oven off; return the cake to the oven for an additional 1 hour. Chill, uncovered, overnight. Makes 12 to 18 slices.

Caramel Apple Cheesecake

Autumn's favorite flavors are harvested in this mouth-watering cheesecake.

Graham Cracker Crust

1 1/4 cups	graham cracker crumbs
3 tablespoons	sugar
1/4 teaspoon	ground cinnamon
1/4 cup	butter or margarine, melted

In a small bowl stir together crumbs, sugar, and cinnamon. Add melted butter or margarine. Stir till well combined. Press crumb mixture evenly onto the bottom of a greased 9-inch springform pan. Set aside.

Caramel Apple Filling

1 cup	apple pie filling
1 large	apple; cored, peeled, and chopped
24 ounces	cream cheese
2/3 cup	dark brown sugar
5 teaspoons	flour
3	eggs
1	egg yolk
1 1/4 teaspoons	ground cinnamon
1 1/4 teaspoons	vanilla extract
3/4 teaspoon	ground nutmeg
2/3 cup	whipping cream or sour cream

In a small bowl stir together pie filling and chopped apple. Set aside. In a large bowl combine cream cheese, brown sugar, and flour. Beat with an electric mixer till smooth. Add eggs and egg yolk, one at a time, beating well after each addition. Beat in cinnamon, vanilla extract, and nutmeg. Stir in whipping cream or sour cream.

Pour half of the cream cheese mixture over the crust. Spoon on 1 cup of the apple mixture. Pour the remaining cream cheese mixture over the apple mixture. Top with the remaining apple mixture. Without disturbing the crust, swirl the blade of a knife through the filling to distribute the fruit evenly.

Bake at 350° for 15 minutes. Lower the temperature to 225° and bake for 1 hour and 10 minutes or until the center no longer looks wet or shiny. Remove the cake from the oven and run a knife around the inside edge of the pan. Turn the oven off; return the cake to the oven for an additional 2 hours. Chill, uncovered, overnight.

Fresh Apple Topping

1 medium	apple, thinly sliced
1 tablespoon	lemon juice
	Dark brown sugar

In a small bowl toss together sliced apple and lemon juice. Sprinkle a thin layer of brown sugar over the top of the cheesecake. Arrange apple slices on top. Chill till serving time. Makes 12 to 18 slices.

Caramel Pecan Cheesecake

Of all the delectable cheesecakes in the book, there's a very good chance that this one will become your all-time favorite.

Homemade Cookie Crust

3/4 cup	flour
2 1/2 tablespoons	sugar
1	egg, lightly beaten
1/4 cup	butter or margarine, softened
1/2 teaspoon	vanilla extract

In a medium bowl stir together flour and sugar. Add egg, butter or margarine, and vanilla extract. Beat with an electric mixer till well combined. With generously greased fingers, press the dough evenly onto the bottom of a greased 9-inch springform pan.

Bake at 350° for 12 to 15 minutes or till lightly browned. Remove from oven and set aside.

Refrigerated Cookie Dough Crust: In place of Homemade Cookie Crust, use 8 ounces of refrigerated sugar cookie dough. Slice dough according to package directions. Arrange dough slices in pan, starting on the outside edge and working your way into the middle. Press dough evenly onto the bottom of the pan. Bake as directed above.

Caramel Pecan Filling

24 ounces	cream cheese
3/4 cup	dark brown sugar
1/3 cup	dark corn syrup
5 teaspoons	cornstarch
3	eggs
1	egg yolk
2 teaspoons	vanilla extract
2/3 cup	chopped pecans

In a large bowl combine cream cheese, brown sugar, corn syrup, and cornstarch. Beat with an electric mixer till smooth. Add eggs and egg yolk, one at a time, beating well after each addition. Beat in vanilla extract. Stir in pecans. Pour the cream cheese mixture over the crust.

Bake at 350° for 15 minutes. Lower the temperature to 225° and bake for 1 hour and 15 minutes or till the center no longer looks wet or shiny. Remove the cake from the oven and run a knife around the inside edge of the pan. Turn the oven off; return the cake to the oven for an additional 1 hour. Chill, uncovered, overnight.

Pecan Frosting

4 teaspoons	butter or margarine
1/3 cup	dark brown sugar
1 1/2 tablespoons	milk
1 1/4 teaspoons	cream of tartar
1/2 teaspoon	vanilla extract
3/4 cup	powdered sugar
	Milk
	Pecan halves

In a small saucepan melt butter or margarine. Stir in brown sugar, 1 1/2 tablespoons milk, and cream of tartar; bring to a boil. Remove from heat and cool to lukewarm (about 110°). Stir in the vanilla extract. Add powdered sugar. Beat with an electric mixer till smooth. Beat in additional milk, 1 tablespoon at a time, till desired consistency. Spread warm frosting over cheesecake. Arrange pecan halves on frosting. Chill till serving time. Makes 12 to 18 slices.

Molasses Cheesecake

Brown sugar and molasses provide the flavor in this crumb-topped cheesecake that tastes like shoofly pie.

Homemade Cookie Crust

3/4 cup	flour
2 1/2 tablespoons	sugar
1	egg, lightly beaten
1/4 cup	butter or margarine, softened
1/2 teaspoon	vanilla extract

In a medium bowl stir together flour and sugar. Add egg, butter or margarine, and vanilla extract. Beat with an electric mixer till well combined. With generously greased fingers, press the dough evenly onto the bottom of a greased 9-inch springform pan.

Bake at 350° for 12 to 15 minutes or till lightly browned. Remove from oven and set aside.

Oatmeal Cookie Crust: In place of Homemade Cookie Crust, crush 22 2-inch oatmeal cookies. Stir in 3 tablespoons melted butter or margarine. Press the crumb mixture evenly onto the bottom of the pan. Set aside.

Molasses Crumb Filling

24 ounces	cream cheese
2/3 cup	dark brown sugar
1/3 cup	unsulphured molasses
5 teaspoons	cornstarch
1/2 teaspoon	baking soda
3	eggs
1	egg yolk
2 teaspoons	vanilla extract
3 tablespoons	butter or margarine
1/3 cup	flour
1/3 cup	dark brown sugar
3 tablespoons	rolled oats

In a large bowl combine cream cheese, 2/3 cup brown sugar, molasses, cornstarch, and baking soda. Beat with an electric mixer till smooth. Add eggs and egg yolk, one at a time, beating well after each addition. Beat in vanilla extract. Set aside.

For crumb topping, in a small saucepan melt butter or margarine. Stir in flour, 1/3 cup brown sugar, and rolled oats till the mixture resembles coarse crumbs. Pour the cream cheese mixture over the crust. Sprinkle with the crumb topping.

Bake at 350° for 15 minutes. Lower the temperature to 200° and bake for 1 hour and 10 minutes or until the center no longer looks wet or shiny. Remove the cake from the oven and run a knife around the inside edge of the pan. Turn the oven off; return the cake to the oven for an additional 1 hour. Chill, uncovered, overnight. Makes 12 to 18 slices.

Caramel Mocha Cheesecake

Caramel, chocolate, and coffee lovers beware . . . this cheesecake is loaded!

Chocolate Cookie Crust

11	milk chocolate sandwich cream cookies, crushed
3 tablespoons	butter or margarine, melted

In a small bowl stir together crushed cookies and melted butter or margarine till well combined. Press crumb mixture evenly onto the bottom of a greased 9-inch springform pan.

Caramel Mocha Filling

24 ounces	cream cheese
1/3 cup	dark brown sugar
5 teaspoons	cornstarch
3	eggs
1	egg yolk
1/3 cup	sour cream
1 1/4 teaspoons	vanilla extract
2 1/2 teaspoons	instant coffee
2 1/2 teaspoons	hot water
2 1/2 tablespoons	sugar
1 3/4 cups	milk chocolate chips, melted
1/4 cup	dark corn syrup

In a large bowl combine cream cheese, brown sugar, and cornstarch. Beat with an electric mixer till smooth. Add eggs and egg yolk, one at a time, beating well after each addition. Stir in sour cream and vanilla extract. Stir together instant coffee and hot water; set aside.

Place 3/4 cup of the cream cheese mixture in a small bowl; add the dissolved coffee. Stir in sugar. Stir melted chocolate chips and corn syrup into remaining cheese mixture.

Pour half of the chocolate mixture over the crust. Spoon 1/2 cup of the coffee mixture over the chocolate mixture. Pour the remaining chocolate mixture over the coffee mixture. Spoon on the remaining coffee mixture. Without disturbing the crust, swirl the blade of a knife through the filling to create a marbling effect.

Bake at 350° for 15 minutes. Lower the temperature to 225° and bake for 1 hour and 10 minutes or until the center no longer looks wet or shiny. Remove the cake from the oven and run a knife around the inside edge of the pan. Turn the oven off; return the cake to the oven for an additional 30 minutes. Chill, uncovered, overnight.

Mocha Sour Cream Topping

1 1/2 teaspoons	hot water
1 1/4 teaspoons	instant coffee
2 1/2 tablespoons	dark brown sugar
1/2 cup	milk chocolate chips, melted
1/4 cup	sour cream

In a small bowl stir together hot water and coffee crystals. Stir in brown sugar. Add melted chocolate chips and sour cream. Stir till well combined. Spread the warm sour cream mixture over the cheesecake. Chill till serving time. Makes 12 to 18 slices.

Chocolate Caramel Pecan Cheesecake

This rich and nutty cheesecake tastes just like a candy bar.

Chocolate Pecan Crust

11	milk chocolate sandwich cream cookies, crushed
3 tablespoons	chopped pecans
3 tablespoons	butter or margarine, melted

In a small bowl stir together crushed cookies and chopped pecans. Stir in melted butter or margarine till well combined. Press crumb mixture evenly onto the bottom of a greased 9-inch springform pan.

Chocolate Caramel Pecan Filling

24 ounces	cream cheese
1/3 cup	dark brown sugar
1/4 cup	dark corn syrup
2 tablespoons	cornstarch
3	eggs
1	egg yolk
1/3 cup	sour cream
1 1/4 teaspoons	vanilla extract
1 3/4 cups	milk chocolate chips, melted
1/3 cup	chopped pecans

In a large bowl combine cream cheese, brown sugar, corn syrup, and cornstarch. Beat with an electric mixer till smooth. Add eggs and egg yolk, one at a time, beating well after each addition. Stir in sour cream and vanilla extract. Stir in melted chocolate chips and pecans. Pour cream cheese mixture over crust.

Bake at 350° for 15 minutes. Lower the temperature to 200° and bake for 1 hour and 10 minutes or until the center no longer looks wet or shiny. Remove the cake from the oven and run a knife around the inside edge of the pan. Turn the oven off; return the cake to the oven for an additional 1 hour. Chill, uncovered, overnight.

Chocolate Caramel Topping

³/₄ cup	milk chocolate chips
¹/₄ cup	sour cream
1 tablespoon	dark brown sugar
3 tablespoons	chopped pecans
	Pecan halves
10	individually wrapped vanilla caramels
2 tablespoons	sour cream

In a small saucepan melt chocolate chips over low heat, stirring constantly. Remove from heat and stir in the ¹/₄ cup sour cream and brown sugar. Stir in pecans. Spread warm sour cream mixture over cheesecake. Arrange pecan halves on top. In a double boiler melt caramels over boiling water. Stir in the 2 tablespoons sour cream. Drizzle caramel mixture over cheesecake. Chill till serving time. Makes 12 to 18 slices.

Chocolate Cheesecakes

Chocolate Cheesecake

This creamy chocolate cheesecake is enveloped in chocolate glaze and garnished with fresh raspberries and chocolate leaves.

Chocolate Wafer Crust

1¼ cups	finely crushed chocolate wafers
3 tablespoons	sugar
¼ cup	butter or margarine, melted

In a small bowl stir together crumbs and sugar. Add melted butter or margarine. Stir till well combined. Press crumb mixture evenly onto the bottom of a greased 9-inch springform pan. Set aside.

Chocolate Filling

24 ounces	cream cheese
¾ cup	sugar
5 teaspoons	cornstarch
4	eggs
1	egg yolk
12 ounces	semisweet chocolate chips, melted
¾ cup	sour cream
1¼ teaspoons	vanilla extract

In a large bowl combine cream cheese, sugar, and cornstarch. Beat with an electric mixer till smooth. Add eggs and egg yolk, one at a time, beating well after each addition. Beat in melted chocolate, sour cream, and vanilla extract. Pour the cream cheese mixture over the crust.

Bake at 350° for 15 minutes. Lower the temperature to 200° and bake for 1 hour and 10 minutes or till the center no longer looks wet or shiny. Remove the cake from the oven and run a knife around the inside edge of the pan. Turn the oven off; return the cake to the oven for an additional 1 hour. Chill, uncovered, overnight.

Chocolate Glaze

12 ounces	semisweet chocolate chips
2 tablespoons	shortening
	Fresh raspberries
	Chocolate leaves

In a small saucepan melt chocolate chips and shortening over low heat, stirring constantly. Spread over top and sides of cheesecake. Garnish with fresh raspberries and chocolate leaves. Chill till serving time. Makes 12 to 18 slices.

Chocolate leaves: Use nontoxic, fresh leaves such as strawberry, mint, lemon, or ivy leaves. Using a small paintbrush, brush melted chocolate on the underside of clean leaves. Place on a baking sheet lined with waxed paper and chill till chocolate hardens. Just before using, peel leaf away from chocolate.

Black Bottom Cheesecake

This delectable cheesecake is flavored with semisweet chocolate and a hint of rum.

Chocolate Cookie Crust

11	chocolate sandwich cream cookies, crushed
3 tablespoons	butter or margarine, melted

In a small bowl stir together crushed cookies and melted butter or margarine till well combined. Press crumb mixture evenly onto the bottom of a greased 9-inch springform pan.

Black Bottom Filling

24 ounces	cream cheese
2/3 cup	sugar
5 teaspoons	cornstarch
2 tablespoons	sour cream
3	eggs
1	egg yolk
1 cup	semisweet chocolate chips, melted
1/4 cup	light rum
2 teaspoons	vanilla extract
2/3 cup	whipping cream

In a large bowl combine cream cheese, sugar, cornstarch, and sour cream. Beat with an electric mixer till smooth. Add eggs and egg yolk, one at a time, beating well after each addition. Beat in melted chocolate, light rum, and vanilla extract. Stir in whipping cream. Pour the cream cheese mixture over the crust.

Bake at 350° for 15 minutes. Lower the temperature to 200° and bake for 1 hour and 10 minutes or till the center no longer looks wet or shiny. Remove the cake from the oven and run a knife around the inside edge of the pan. Turn the oven off; return the cake to the oven for an additional 1 hour. Chill, uncovered, overnight.

Fluffy Chocolate Rum Topping

1 cup	whipping cream
2 tablespoons	powdered sugar
1 tablespoon	unsweetened cocoa powder
1 tablespoon	light rum
	Chocolate curls (optional)

In a small bowl beat whipping cream, powdered sugar, cocoa powder, and rum with an electric mixer till stiff peaks form. Pipe whipped cream mixture around the edge of the cheesecake. Garnish with chocolate curls, if desired. Chill till serving time. Makes 12 to 18 slices.

Black Forest Cheesecake

Sometimes it takes this cheesecake longer than 1 hour to set in the turned-off oven until it no longer looks shiny. Be patient . . . this chocolate and cherry dessert is well worth the wait.

Chocolate Wafer Crust

1 1/4 cups	finely crushed chocolate wafers
3 tablespoons	sugar
1/4 cup	butter or margarine, melted

In a small bowl stir together crumbs and sugar. Add melted butter or margarine. Stir till well combined. Press crumb mixture evenly onto the bottom of a greased 9-inch springform pan. Set aside.

Black Forest Filling

24 ounces	cream cheese
3/4 cup	sugar
5 teaspoons	cornstarch
3	eggs
1	egg yolk
1 cup	semisweet chocolate chips, melted
1/2 cup	cherry schnapps
2 teaspoons	vanilla extract
2/3 cup	bing cherries, pitted, chopped, and drained

In a large bowl combine cream cheese, sugar, and cornstarch. Beat with an electric mixer till smooth. Add eggs and egg yolk, one at a time, beating well after each addition. Beat in melted chocolate, cherry schnapps, and vanilla extract. Stir in cherries. Pour the cream cheese mixture over the crust.

Bake at 350° for 15 minutes. Lower the temperature to 200° and bake for 1 hour and 10 minutes or till the center no longer looks wet or shiny. Remove the cake from the oven and run a knife around the inside edge of the pan. Turn the oven off; return the cake to the oven for an additional 1 hour. Chill, uncovered, overnight.

Chocolate Cherry Topping

1 cup	cherry preserves
2 teaspoons	lemon juice
1 teaspoon	cornstarch
	Chocolate ice cream topping

In a small saucepan stir together cherry preserves, lemon juice, and cornstarch. Cook and stir till thickened and bubbly. Cook and stir 2 minutes more. Pour over cheesecake. Drizzle with chocolate ice cream topping. Chill till serving time. Makes 12 to 18 slices.

Chocolate Banana Cheesecake

This interesting cheesecake has a chocolate crust, chocolate swirled banana filling, and chocolate topping.

Chocolate Cookie Crust

11	chocolate sandwich cream cookies, crushed
3 tablespoons	butter or margarine, melted

In a small bowl stir together crushed cookies and melted butter or margarine till well combined. Press crumb mixture evenly onto the bottom of a greased 9-inch springform pan.

Chocolate Banana Filling

24 ounces	cream cheese
3/4 cup	sugar
5 teaspoons	cornstarch
3	eggs
1	egg yolk
1 1/4 teaspoons	vanilla extract
3 tablespoons	sugar
2 tablespoons	unsweetened cocoa powder
2/3 cup	puréed bananas (2 small bananas)
1/2 cup	banana schnapps

In a large bowl combine cream cheese, 3/4 cup sugar, and cornstarch. Beat with an electric mixer till smooth. Add eggs and egg yolk, one at a time, beating well after each addition. Beat in vanilla extract.

Remove 3/4 cup of the mixture and put into a small bowl; stir in 3 tablespoons sugar and cocoa powder. Set aside. Stir puréed banana and banana schnapps into the remaining cream cheese mixture.

Pour half of the banana mixture over the crust. Spoon 1/2 cup of the cocoa mixture over the banana mixture. Pour the remaining banana mixture over the cocoa mixture. Top with remaining cocoa mixture. Without disturbing the crust, swirl the blade of a knife through the cake to create a marbling effect.

Bake at 350° for 15 minutes. Lower the temperature to 225° and bake for 1 hour and 10 minutes or till the center no longer looks wet or shiny. Remove the cake from the oven and run a knife around the inside edge of the pan. Chill, uncovered, overnight.

Chocolate Pecan Topping

1/2 cup	semisweet chocolate chips
3 tablespoons	sour cream
2 tablespoons	powdered sugar
3 tablespoons	chopped pecans

In a small saucepan melt chocolate chips over low heat, stirring constantly. Stir in sour cream and powdered sugar till smooth. Spread over cheesecake. Sprinkle with pecans. Chill till serving time. Makes 12 to 18 slices.

Mocha Almond Swirl Cheesecake

This show-stopping cheesecake has 3 swirled flavors . . . coffee, amaretto, and crème de cacao.

Chocolate Almond Cookie Crust

11	milk chocolate sandwich cream cookies, crushed
3 tablespoons	chopped almonds, toasted
3 tablespoons	butter or margarine, melted

In a small bowl stir together crushed cookies, chopped almonds, and melted butter or margarine till well combined. Press crumb mixture evenly onto the bottom of a greased 9-inch springform pan.

Mocha Almond Filling

24 ounces	cream cheese
3/4 cup	sugar
5 teaspoons	cornstarch
4	large eggs
1	egg yolk
1/4 cup	whipping cream
1 teaspoon	vanilla extract
1 teaspoon	instant coffee
1 teaspoon	hot water
1/4 cup	coffee-flavored liqueur
1/4 cup	amaretto
1/4 cup	crème de cacao
3 tablespoons	sugar
2 tablespoons	unsweetened cocoa powder

In a large bowl combine cream cheese, 3/4 cup sugar, and cornstarch. Beat with an electric mixer till smooth. Add eggs and egg yolk, one at a time, beating well after each addition. Beat in whipping cream and vanilla extract.

Stir together instant coffee and hot water till dissolved. Remove 1 1/4 cups of the cream cheese mixture and put into a small bowl; stir in coffee and coffee-flavored liqueur. Set aside. Remove another 1 1/4 cups of the cream cheese mixture. Stir in amaretto. Set aside. Stir the crème de cacao, the 3 tablespoons sugar, and cocoa powder into the remaining cream cheese mixture.

Pour the cocoa mixture over the crust. Spoon coffee mixture over the cocoa mixture. Pour the amaretto mixture over the cocoa mixture. Without disturbing the crust, swirl the blade of a knife through the cake to create a marbling effect.

Bake at 350° for 15 minutes. Lower the temperature to 200° and bake for 1 hour and 10 minutes or till the center no longer looks wet or shiny. Remove the cake from the oven and run a knife around the inside edge of the pan. Turn the oven off; return the cake to the oven for an additional 1 hour. Chill, uncovered, overnight. Makes 12 to 18 slices.

Chocolate Mint Swirl Cheesecake

This colorful cheesecake has 3 layers that are attractively marbled together.

Chocolate Cookie Crust

| 11 | chocolate sandwich cream cookies, crushed |
| 3 tablespoons | butter or margarine, melted |

In a small bowl stir together crushed cookies and melted butter or margarine till well combined. Press crumb mixture evenly onto the bottom of a greased 9-inch springform pan.

Chocolate Mint Filling

24 ounces	cream cheese
3/4 cup	sugar
3 tablespoons	whipping cream
5 teaspoons	cornstarch
4	eggs
1	egg yolk
1 teaspoon	vanilla extract
3 tablespoons	crème de menthe
3 tablespoons	rum
1 tablespoon	whipping cream
3 tablespoons	crème de cacao
2 tablespoons	sugar
1 tablespoon	unsweetened cocoa powder

In a large bowl combine cream cheese, ³/₄ cup sugar, 3 tablespoons whipping cream, and cornstarch. Beat with an electric mixer till smooth. Add eggs and egg yolk, one at a time, beating well after each addition. Beat in vanilla extract.

Remove 1¼ cups of the mixture and put into a small bowl; stir in creme de menthe. Set aside. Remove another 1¼ cups of the mixture and put into a small bowl; stir in rum and 1 tablespoon whipping cream. Set aside. Stir crème de cacao, 2 tablespoons sugar, and cocoa powder into the remaining cream cheese mixture.

Pour the cocoa mixture over the crust. Spoon ²/₃ cup of the cocoa mixture over the amaretto mixture. Pour the crème de menthe mixture over the cocoa mixture. Top with the rum mixture. Without disturbing the crust, swirl the blade of a knife through the cake to create a marbling effect.

Bake at 350° for 15 minutes. Lower the temperature to 200° and bake for 1 hour and 10 minutes or till the center no longer looks wet or shiny. Remove the cake from the oven and run a knife around the inside edge of the pan. Turn the oven off; return the cake to the oven for an additional 1 hour. Chill, uncovered, overnight.

Crème de Menthe Topping

1 cup	whipping cream
1 tablespoon	sugar
1 tablespoon	crème de menthe
	Chocolate-covered mints

In a small bowl beat whipping cream, sugar, and crème de menthe with an electric mixer till stiff peaks form. Pipe whipped cream mixture around the edge of the cheesecake. Garnish with chocolate-covered mints. Chill till serving time. Makes 12 to 18 slices.

Chocolate Orange and Almond Swirl Cheesecake

Chocolate Cookie Crust

11	milk chocolate sandwich cream cookies, crushed
3 tablespoons	butter or margarine, melted

In a small bowl stir together crushed cookies and melted butter or margarine till well combined. Press crumb mixture evenly onto the bottom of a greased 9-inch springform pan.

Chocolate Orange and Amaretto Filling

24 ounces	cream cheese
²/₃ cup	sugar
3 tablespoons	whipping cream
5 teaspoons	cornstarch
4	eggs
1	egg yolk
3 tablespoons	orange schnapps
1 teaspoon	finely shredded orange peel
3 tablespoons	amaretto
1 teaspoon	almond extract
3 tablespoons	crème de cacao
2½ tablespoons	unsweetened cocoa powder
2½ tablespoons	sugar

In a large bowl combine cream cheese, ²/₃ cup sugar, whipping cream, and cornstarch. Beat with an electric mixer till smooth. Add eggs and egg yolk, one at a time, beating well after each addition.

Remove 1¼ cups of the mixture and put into a small bowl; stir in orange schnapps and orange peel. Set aside. Remove another 1¼ cups of the mixture and put into a small bowl; stir in amaretto and almond extract. Stir crème de cacao, cocoa powder, and 2½ tablespoons sugar into the remaining cream cheese mixture.

Pour the cocoa mixture over the crust. Spoon the orange mixture over the cocoa mixture. Top with amaretto mixture. Without disturbing the crust, swirl the blade of a knife through the cake to create a marbling effect.

Bake at 350° for 15 minutes. Lower the temperature to 200° and bake for 1 hour and 10 minutes or till the center no longer looks wet or shiny. Remove the cake from the oven and run a knife around the inside edge of the pan. Chill, uncovered, overnight.

Chocolate Orange Topping

½ cup	semisweet chocolate chips
3 tablespoons	sour cream
2 tablespoons	powdered sugar
1 teaspoon	finely shredded orange peel
1 tablespoon	orange juice
	Whole almonds

In a small saucepan melt chocolate chips over low heat, stirring constantly. Stir in sour cream, powdered sugar, orange peel, and orange juice till smooth. Spread over cheesecake. Garnish with almonds. Chill till serving time. Makes 12 to 18 slices.

Chocolate Orange Cheesecake

Chocolate Cookie Crust

11	chocolate sandwich cream cookies, crushed
3 tablespoons	butter or margarine, melted

In a small bowl stir together crushed cookies and melted butter or margarine till well combined. Press crumb mixture evenly onto the bottom of a greased 9-inch springform pan.

Chocolate Orange Filling

24 ounces	cream cheese
³/₄ cup	sugar
5 teaspoons	cornstarch
3	eggs
1	egg yolk
¹/₂ cup	orange schnapps
¹/₃ cup	frozen orange juice concentrate, thawed
1 teaspoon	finely shredded orange peel
1 teaspoon	vanilla extract
	Orange food coloring (optional)

In a large bowl combine cream cheese, ³/₄ cup sugar, and cornstarch. Beat with an electric mixer till smooth. Add eggs and egg yolk, one at a time, beating well after each addition. Beat in orange schnapps, orange juice concentrate, orange peel, and vanilla extract. Stir in food coloring, if desired. Pour cream cheese mixture over crust.

Bake at 350° for 15 minutes. Lower the temperature to 225° and bake for 1 hour and 10 minutes or till the center no longer looks wet or shiny. Remove the cake from the oven and run a knife around the inside edge of the pan. Turn the oven off; return the cake to the oven for an additional 30 minutes. Chill, uncovered, overnight.

Chocolate Topping

1 cup	semisweet chocolate chips
1 tablespoon	sour cream
	Pecan halves

In a small saucepan melt chocolate over low heat, stirring constantly. Stir in sour cream. Drizzle over cheesecake. Garnish with pecans. Chill till serving time. Makes 12 to 18 slices.

Chocolate Mousse Cheesecake

This chocolate cheesecake gets its extra richness from sour cream, whipping cream, and 2 kinds of chocolate.

Chocolate Cookie Crust

11	milk chocolate sandwich cream cookies, crushed
3 tablespoons	butter or margarine, melted

In a small bowl stir together crushed cookies and melted butter or margarine till well combined. Press crumb mixture evenly onto the bottom of a greased 9-inch springform pan.

Chocolate Mousse Filling

19 ounces	cream cheese
1 cup	sour cream
³/₄ cup	sugar
5	eggs
10 ounces	milk chocolate chips, melted
1 ¹/₄ teaspoons	vanilla extract
¹/₂ cup	whipping cream
3 ounces	German sweet chocolate, grated

In a large bowl combine cream cheese, sour cream, and sugar. Beat with an electric mixer till smooth. Add eggs, one at a time, beating well after each addition. Beat in melted chocolate and vanilla extract. Stir in whipping cream and grated chocolate. Pour the cream cheese mixture over the crust.

Bake at 350° for 15 minutes. Lower the temperature to 200° and bake for 1 hour and 25 minutes or till the center no longer looks wet or shiny. Remove the cake from the oven and run a knife around the inside edge of the pan. Turn the oven off; return the cake to the oven for an additional 2 hours. Chill, uncovered, overnight. Makes 12 to 18 slices.

Chocolate Peanut Butter Cheesecake

There's a good chance that many of you will indulge in this outstanding cheesecake time after luscious time.

Chocolate Peanut Cookie Crust

11	chocolate sandwich cream cookies, crushed
3 tablespoons	chopped peanuts
3 tablespoons	butter or margarine, melted

In a small bowl stir together crushed cookies and peanuts. Stir in melted butter or margarine till well combined. Press crumb mixture evenly onto the bottom of a greased 9-inch springform pan.

Chocolate Peanut Butter Filling

19 ounces	cream cheese
1 cup	sour cream
2/3 cup	dark brown sugar
5 teaspoons	cornstarch
4	eggs
1	egg yolk
2/3 cup	whipping cream
1 1/4 teaspoons	vanilla extract
2 1/2 tablespoons	sugar
5 teaspoons	unsweetened cocoa powder
1 1/4 cups	creamy peanut butter
2/3 cup	chopped peanuts

In a large bowl combine cream cheese, sour cream, brown sugar, and cornstarch. Beat with an electric mixer till smooth. Add eggs and egg yolk, one at a time, beating well after each addition. Stir in whipping cream and vanilla extract.

Remove 1 cup of the mixture and put into a small bowl; stir in sugar and cocoa powder. Set aside. Stir peanut butter and chopped peanuts into the remaining cream cheese mixture.

Pour half of the peanut butter mixture over the crust. Spoon half of the cocoa mixture over the peanut butter mixture. Pour the remaining peanut butter mixture over the cocoa mixture. Top with remaining cocoa mixture. Without disturbing the crust, swirl the blade of a knife through the cake to create a marbling effect.

Bake at 350° for 15 minutes. Lower the temperature to 200° and bake for 1 hour and 10 minutes or till the center no longer looks wet or shiny. Remove the cake from the oven and run a knife around the inside edge of the pan. Chill, uncovered, overnight.

Hot Peanut Butter Fudge Topping

3/4 cup	semisweet chocolate chips
1/4 cup	butter or margarine
2/3 cup	sugar
1 5-ounce can (2/3 cup)	evaporated milk
1/4 cup	peanut butter

In a small saucepan melt chocolate and butter or margarine over low heat, stirring constantly. Add the sugar. Gradually stir in milk. Bring to a boil; reduce heat. Simmer, uncovered, for 8 minutes, stirring frequently. Stir in peanut butter till smooth. Remove from heat. Serve warm with cheesecake. Makes 12 to 18 slices.

Chocolate Toffee Cheesecake

This sophisticated cheesecake boasts a shortbread cookie crust, a rich mocha filling, and a hot fudge topping.

Pecan Shortbread Crust

1 1/4 cups	pecan shortbread cookie crumbs
1/4 cup	chopped pecans
1/4 cup	butter or margarine, melted

In a small bowl stir together crumbs and pecans. Add melted butter or margarine. Stir till well combined. Press crumb mixture evenly onto the bottom of a greased 9-inch springform pan. Set aside.

Chocolate Toffee Filling

19 ounces	cream cheese
1 1/4 cups	sour cream
4	eggs
1 1/4 teaspoons	vanilla extract
1/2 teaspoon	instant coffee
1/2 teaspoon	hot water
1/4 cup	dark brown sugar
1 cup	milk chocolate chips, melted
1 cup	semisweet chocolate chips, melted
1/2 cup	sugar

In a large bowl combine cream cheese and sour cream. Beat with an electric mixer till smooth. Add eggs, one at a time, beating well after each addition. Beat in vanilla extract.

Stir together coffee and hot water. Stir in brown sugar. Remove half of the cream cheese mixture and put into a small bowl; stir in coffee mixture and melted milk chocolate. Set aside. Stir melted semisweet chocolate and sugar into the remaining cream cheese mixture.

Pour the semisweet chocolate mixture over the crust. Top with the milk chocolate mixture.

Bake at 350° for 15 minutes. Lower the temperature to 200° and bake for 1 hour and 10 minutes or till the center no longer looks wet or shiny. Remove the cake from the oven and run a knife around the inside edge of the pan. Turn the oven off; return the cake to the oven for an additional 2 hours. Chill, uncovered, overnight.

Hot Fudge Topping

³/₄ cup	semisweet chocolate chips
¹/₄ cup	butter or margarine
²/₃ cup	sugar
1 5-ounce can (²/₃ cup)	evaporated milk
¹/₄ cup	chopped chocolate-covered toffee candy bar

In a small saucepan melt chocolate and butter or margarine over low heat, stirring constantly. Add the sugar. Gradually stir in milk. Bring to a boil; reduce heat. Simmer, uncovered, for 8 minutes, stirring frequently. Remove from heat. Serve warm with cheesecake. Garnish with chopped toffee bars. Makes 12 to 18 slices.

Chocolate Fantasy Cheesecake

This ultimate cheesecake is a chocolate lover's dream come true. Make it when you really want to impress someone.

Chocolate Cookie Crust

11	chocolate sandwich cream cookies, crushed
3 tablespoons	butter or margarine, melted

In a small bowl stir together crushed cookies and melted butter or margarine till well combined. Press crumb mixture evenly onto the bottom of a greased 9-inch springform pan.

Double Chocolate Filling

19 ounces	cream cheese
²/₃ cup	sugar
5	eggs
¹/₂ cup	sour cream
¹/₂ cup	whipping cream
¹/₃ cup	crème de cacao
1 ¹/₄ teaspoons	vanilla extract
10 ounces	semisweet chocolate, melted
3 ounces	German sweet chocolate, grated

In a large bowl combine cream cheese and sugar. Beat with an electric mixer till smooth. Add eggs, one at a time, beating well after each addition. Stir in sour cream, whipping cream, crème de cacao, and vanilla extract. Stir in melted semisweet chocolate and grated German chocolate. Pour the cream cheese mixture over the crust.

Bake at 350° for 15 minutes. Lower the temperature to 200° and bake for 1 hour and 10 minutes or till the center no longer looks wet or shiny. Remove the cake from the oven and run a knife around the inside edge of the pan. Turn the oven off; return the cake to the oven for an additional 2 hours. Chill, uncovered, overnight. Makes 12 to 18 slices.

German Chocolate Cheesecake

If you're a fan of German chocolate cake, you'll love this cheesecake version.

Homemade Chocolate Cookie Crust

³/₄ cup	flour
¹/₄ cup	sugar
4 teaspoons	unsweetened cocoa powder
1	egg, lightly beaten
5 tablespoons	butter or margarine, softened
³/₄ teaspoon	vanilla extract

In a medium bowl stir together flour, sugar, and cocoa powder. Add egg, butter or margarine, and vanilla extract. Beat with an electric mixer till well combined. With generously greased fingers, press the dough evenly onto the bottom of a greased 9-inch springform pan.

Bake at 350° for 12 to 15 minutes or till lightly browned. Remove from oven and set aside.

German Chocolate Filling

24 ounces	cream cheese
³/₄ cup	sugar
¹/₂ cup	sour cream
3	eggs
1	egg yolk
1 ¹/₄ teaspoons	vanilla extract
7 ounces	German sweet chocolate, melted

In a large bowl combine cream cheese, sugar, and sour cream. Beat with an electric mixer till smooth. Add eggs and egg yolk, one at a time, beating well after each addition. Beat in vanilla extract. Stir in melted chocolate. Pour the cream cheese mixture over the crust.

Bake at 350° for 15 minutes. Lower the temperature to 200° and bake for 1 hour and 10 minutes or till the center no longer looks wet or shiny. Remove the cake from the oven and run a knife around the inside edge of the pan. Chill, uncovered, overnight.

Coconut Pecan Topping

¹/₄ cup	butter or margarine
¹/₃ cup	sugar
¹/₃ cup	evaporated milk
1	egg yolk, lightly beaten
1 cup	flaked coconut
¹/₂ cup	chopped pecans
1 ¹/₄ teaspoons	vanilla extract
	Pecan halves
	Chocolate curls

In a small saucepan melt the butter or margarine. Stir in sugar, evaporated milk, and egg yolk. Cook and stir over low heat about 10 minutes or until thickened. Stir in ²/₃ cup of the coconut, chopped pecans, and vanilla extract. Spread over the cake. Garnish with remaining coconut, pecan halves, and chocolate curls. Chill till serving time. Makes 12 to 18 slices.

Milk Chocolate Cheesecake

This is just like eating a big milk chocolate candy bar, only better.

Chocolate Cookie Crust

11	milk chocolate sandwich cream cookies, crushed
3 tablespoons	butter or margarine, melted

In a small bowl stir together crushed cookies and melted butter or margarine till well combined. Press crumb mixture evenly onto the bottom of a greased 9-inch springform pan.

Milk Chocolate Filling

24 ounces	cream cheese
3/4 cup	sugar
3/4 cup	sour cream
4	eggs
1 1/4 teaspoons	vanilla extract
1 12-ounce package	milk chocolate chips, melted

In a large bowl combine cream cheese, sugar, and sour cream. Beat with an electric mixer till smooth. Add eggs, one at a time, beating well after each addition. Beat in vanilla extract. Stir in melted chocolate. Pour the cream cheese mixture over the crust.

　Bake at 350° for 15 minutes. Lower the temperature to 200° and bake for 1 hour and 10 minutes or till the center no longer looks wet or shiny. Remove the cake from the oven and run a knife around the inside edge of the pan. Turn the oven off; return the cake to the oven for an additional 2 hours. Chill, uncovered, overnight.

Milk Chocolate Topping

1 cup	whipping cream
1 tablespoon	sugar
1/2 cup	milk chocolate chips

In a small bowl beat whipping cream and sugar with an electric mixer till stiff peaks form. Pipe whipped cream mixture around the edge of the cheesecake. Garnish with milk chocolate chips. Chill till serving time. Makes 12 to 18 slices.

Coconut Cheesecakes

Chocolate Coconut Almond Cheesecake

This multi-flavored cheesecake tastes just like a popular chocolate-covered coconut almond candy bar.

Chocolate Almond Cookie Crust

11	milk chocolate sandwich cream cookies, crushed
3 tablespoons	chopped almonds, toasted
3 tablespoons	butter or margarine, melted

In a small bowl stir together crushed cookies and chopped almonds. Stir in melted butter or margarine till well combined. Press crumb mixture evenly onto the bottom of a greased 9-inch springform pan.

Coconut Almond Filling

24 ounces	cream cheese
3/4 cup	sugar
5 teaspoons	cornstarch
3	eggs
1	egg yolk
1/2 cup	cream of coconut
1 1/4 teaspoons	vanilla extract
1 1/4 teaspoons	almond extract
2/3 cup	flaked or freshly grated coconut
1/4 cup	chopped almonds, toasted

In a large bowl combine cream cheese, sugar, and cornstarch. Beat with an electric mixer till smooth. Add eggs and egg yolk, one at a time, beating well after each addition. Beat in cream of coconut, vanilla extract, and almond extract. Stir in coconut and almonds. Pour the cream cheese mixture over the crust.

Bake at 350° for 15 minutes. Lower the temperature to 225° and bake for 1 hour and 10 minutes or till the center no longer looks wet or shiny. Remove the cake from the oven and run a knife around the inside edge of the pan. Turn the oven off; return the cake to the oven for an additional 1 hour. Chill, uncovered, overnight.

Chocolate Coconut Topping

¹/₂ cup	semisweet or milk chocolate chips
¹/₄ cup	sour cream
2 tablespoons	sugar
	Flaked or freshly grated coconut
	Whole or chopped almonds
	Shaved or grated chocolate or chocolate curls

In a small saucepan melt semisweet or milk chocolate over low heat, stirring constantly. Stir in sour cream and sugar. Spread the warm chocolate mixture over the cake. Garnish with coconut, almonds, and chocolate. Chill till serving time. Makes 12 to 18 slices.

Coconut Pineapple Almond Cheesecake

Toasted Coconut Crust

1³/₄ cups	flaked or freshly grated coconut
4 teaspoons	coarsely chopped almonds, toasted
3 tablespoons	butter or margarine, softened

In a small bowl stir together coconut and almonds. Add butter or margarine and stir till well combined. Press the coconut mixture evenly onto the bottom of a greased 9-inch springform pan. Bake at 350° for 12 to 15 minutes or until golden. Set aside.

Coconut Pineapple Filling

24 ounces	cream cheese
³/₄ cup	sugar
5 teaspoons	cornstarch
3	eggs
1	egg yolk
¹/₂ cup	frozen pineapple juice concentrate, thawed
2 tablespoons	sour cream
2 tablespoons	cream of coconut
2 teaspoons	lemon juice
1 teaspoon	vanilla extract
1 teaspoon	almond extract
1 8-ounce can	crushed pineapple, drained

In a large bowl combine cream cheese, sugar, and cornstarch. Beat with an electric mixer till smooth. Add eggs and egg yolk, one at a time, beating well after each addition. Stir in pineapple juice concentrate, sour cream, cream of coconut, vanilla extract, and almond extract. Stir in pineapple. Pour the cream cheese mixture over the crust.

Bake at 375° for 15 minutes. Lower the temperature to 225° and bake for 1 hour or till the center no longer looks wet or shiny. Remove the cake from the oven and run a knife around the inside edge of the pan. Chill, uncovered, overnight.

Pineapple Glaze

¹/₂ cup	frozen pineapple juice concentrate, thawed
4 teaspoons	lemon juice
1 tablespoon	cornstarch
1 tablespoon	orange juice
	Fresh fruit, sliced

In a small saucepan stir together pineapple juice concentrate, lemon juice, cornstarch, and orange juice. Cook and stir till thickened and bubbly. Cook and stir 2 minutes more. Pour over cheesecake. Garnish with fruit. Chill till serving time. Makes 12 to 18 slices.

Coconut Chocolate Rum Cheesecake

Toasted Coconut Crust

| 1³/₄ cups | flaked or freshly grated coconut |
| 3 tablespoons | butter or margarine, softened |

In a small bowl stir together coconut and butter or margarine till well combined. Press the coconut mixture evenly onto the bottom of a greased 9-inch springform pan. Bake at 350° for 12 to 15 minutes or until golden. Set aside.

Chocolate Rum Filling

19 ounces	cream cheese
³/₄ cup	sugar
1 cup	sour cream
4	eggs
2 tablespoons	rum
1¹/₄ teaspoons	vanilla extract
1 12-ounce package	milk chocolate chips, melted

In a large bowl combine cream cheese, sugar, and sour cream. Beat with an electric mixer till smooth. Add eggs, one at a time, beating well after each addition. Beat in rum and vanilla extract. Stir in melted chocolate. Pour the cream cheese mixture over the crust.

Bake at 350° for 15 minutes. Lower the temperature to 200° and bake for 1 hour and 10 minutes or till the center no longer looks wet or shiny. Remove the cake from the oven and run a knife around the inside edge of the pan. Turn the oven off; return the cake to the oven for an additional 2 hours. Chill, uncovered, overnight.

Warm Coconut Topping

¹/₄ cup	brown sugar
2 tablespoons	butter or margarine, softened
2 tablespoons	milk
¹/₂ cup	flaked coconut

In a bowl beat brown sugar and butter or margarine till combined. Stir in milk. Stir in coconut. Spread over cheesecake. Broil about 4 inches from the heat for 3 to 4 minutes or till golden. Serve warm. Makes 12 to 18 slices.

Coconut Almond Cheesecake

Toasted Coconut Crust

1³/₄ cups	flaked or freshly grated coconut
4 teaspoons	coarsely chopped almonds, toasted
3 tablespoons	butter or margarine, softened

In a small bowl stir together coconut and almonds. Add butter or margarine and stir till well combined. Press the coconut mixture evenly onto the bottom of a greased 9-inch springform pan. Bake at 350° for 12 to 15 minutes or until golden. Set aside.

Coconut Almond Filling

24 ounces	cream cheese
²/₃ cup	sugar
5 teaspoons	cornstarch
3	eggs
1	egg yolk
¹/₂ cup	cream of coconut
1¹/₄ teaspoons	vanilla extract
1¹/₄ teaspoons	almond extract
²/₃ cup	flaked or freshly grated coconut
¹/₄ cup	chopped almonds, toasted

In a large bowl combine cream cheese, sugar, and cornstarch. Beat with an electric mixer till smooth. Add eggs and egg yolk, one at a time, beating well after each addition. Beat in cream of coconut, vanilla extract, and almond extract. Stir in coconut and almonds. Pour the cream cheese mixture over the crust.

Bake at 350° for 15 minutes. Lower the temperature to 225° and bake for 1 hour and 10 minutes or till the center no longer looks wet or shiny. Remove the cake from the oven and run a knife around the inside edge of the pan. Turn the oven off; return the cake to the oven for an additional 1 hour. Chill, uncovered, overnight. Makes 12 to 18 slices.

Custard and Spice Cheesecakes

Pumpkin Cheesecake

Break away from traditional pumpkin pie and serve this festive cheesecake during the holiday season.

Homemade Cookie Crust

³/₄ cup	flour
2¹/₂ tablespoons	sugar
1	egg, lightly beaten
¹/₄ cup	butter or margarine, softened
¹/₂ teaspoon	vanilla extract

In a medium bowl stir together flour and sugar. Add egg, butter or margarine, and vanilla extract. Beat with an electric mixer till well combined. With generously greased fingers, press the dough evenly onto the bottom of a greased 9-inch springform pan.

Bake at 350° for 12 to 15 minutes or till lightly browned. Remove from oven and set aside.

Refrigerated Cookie Dough Crust: In place of Homemade Cookie Crust, use 8 ounces of refrigerated sugar cookie dough. Slice dough according to package directions. Arrange dough slices in pan, starting on the outside edge and working your way into the middle. Press dough evenly onto the bottom of the pan. Bake as directed above.

Pumpkin Filling

24 ounces	cream cheese
¹/₃ cup	dark brown sugar
5 teaspoons	flour
4	eggs
1	egg yolk
¹/₂ 16-oz. can	pumpkin
¹/₂ cup	whipping cream
2 teaspoons	vanilla extract
1 teaspoon	ground cinnamon
¹/₂ teaspoon	ground nutmeg
¹/₂ teaspoon	ground ginger
¹/₂ teaspoon	ground cloves
	Fresh cranberries
	Walnuts
	Orange slices

In a large bowl combine cream cheese, brown sugar, and flour. Beat with an electric mixer till smooth. Add eggs and egg yolk, one at a time, beating well after each addition. Stir in pumpkin, whipping cream, vanilla extract, cinnamon, nutmeg, ginger, and cloves. Pour the cream cheese mixture over the crust.

Bake at 350° for 15 minutes. Lower the temperature to 225° and bake for 1 hour and 15 minutes or till the center no longer looks wet or shiny. Remove the cake from the oven and run a knife around the inside edge of the pan. Turn the oven off; return the cake to the oven for an additional 1 hour. Chill, uncovered, overnight. Garnish with cranberries, walnuts, and orange slices. Chill till serving time. Makes 12 to 18 slices.

Carrot Cheesecake

This carrot orange dessert rates right up there with the all-time favorite carrot cake.

Graham Cracker Crust

1 ¼ cups	graham cracker crumb
3 tablespoons	sugar
¼ teaspoon	ground cinnamon
¼ cup	butter or margarine, melted

In a small bowl stir together crumbs, sugar, and cinnamon. Add melted butter or margarine. Stir till well combined. Press crumb mixture evenly onto the bottom of a greased 9-inch springform pan. Set aside.

Carrot Filling

24 ounces	cream cheese
¾ cup	sugar
5 teaspoons	flour
3	eggs
1	egg yolk
½ cup	frozen orange juice concentrate, thawed
2 medium	carrots, finely shredded
⅔ cup	whipping cream
1 ¼ teaspoons	vanilla extract
1 teaspoon	finely shredded orange peel

In a large bowl combine cream cheese, sugar, and flour. Beat with an electric mixer till smooth. Add eggs and egg yolk, one at a time, beating well after each addition. Stir in orange juice concentrate, shredded carrots, whipping cream, vanilla extract, and orange peel. Pour the cream cheese mixture over the crust.

Bake at 400° for 15 minutes. Lower the temperature to 225° and bake for 1 hour and 10 minutes or till the center no longer looks wet or shiny. Remove the cake from the oven and run a knife around the inside edge of the pan. Chill, uncovered, overnight.

Cinnamon Orange Topping

2 tablespoons	milk
2 tablespoons	butter or margarine
1/2 teaspoon	vanilla extract
1 1/4 cups	sifted powdered sugar
1 teaspoon	finely shredded orange peel
1/2 teaspoon	ground cinnamon
	Fresh orange wedges

In a small saucepan bring milk and butter or margarine to a boil. Remove from heat. Stir in vanilla. In a bowl stir together powdered sugar, orange peel, and cinnamon. Add butter mixture. Beat with an electric mixer till smooth. Spread over cake. Garnish with fresh orange wedges. Chill till serving time. Makes 12 to 18 slices.

Fruit Cheesecakes

Mandarin Orange Cheesecake

Bottoms up! This clever cheesecake is baked in a flan pan, inverted onto a serving plate, and decorated upside down. Your dessert companions will love it!

Graham Cracker Crust

1¼ cups	graham cracker crumbs
3 tablespoons	sugar
¼ teaspoon	ground cinnamon
¼ cup	butter or margarine, melted

In a small bowl stir together crumbs, sugar, and cinnamon. Add melted butter or margarine. Stir till well combined. Press crumb mixture evenly onto the bottom of a greased 9-inch fluted flan pan. Set aside.

Mandarin Orange Filling

24 ounces	cream cheese
¾ cup	sugar
¼ cup	sour cream
5 teaspoons	cornstarch
3	eggs
1	egg yolk
½ cup	frozen orange juice concentrate, thawed
2 teaspoons	vanilla extract
1 11-ounce can	mandarin orange segments, drained
	Fresh fruit

In a large bowl combine cream cheese, sugar, sour cream, and cornstarch. Beat with an electric mixer till smooth. Add eggs and egg yolk, one at a time, beating well after each addition. Beat in orange juice concentrate and vanilla extract. Stir in mandarin orange segments. Pour the cream cheese mixture over the crust.

Bake at 350° for 15 minutes. Lower the temperature to 225° and bake for 1 hour and 10 minutes or till the center no longer looks wet or shiny. Remove the cake from the oven and run a knife around the inside edge of the pan. Chill, uncovered, overnight. Before serving, invert the cheesecake onto a serving plate. Garnish the top of the graham cracker crust with fresh fruit. Chill till serving time. Makes 12 to 18 slices.

Apple Pie Cheesecake

This tasty cheesecake is reminiscent of apple pie thanks to applesauce, apple juice, cinnamon, and nutmeg.

Homemade Cookie Crust

³/₄ cup	flour
2 ¹/₂ tablespoons	sugar
¹/₂ teaspoon	ground cinnamon
1	egg, lightly beaten
¹/₄ cup	butter or margarine, softened
¹/₂ teaspoon	vanilla extract

In a medium bowl stir together flour, sugar, and cinnamon. Add egg, butter or margarine, and vanilla extract. Beat with an electric mixer till well combined. With generously greased fingers, press the dough evenly onto the bottom of a greased 9-inch springform pan.

Bake at 350° for 12 to 15 minutes or till lightly browned. Remove from oven and set aside.

Refrigerated Cookie Dough Crust: In place of Homemade Cookie Crust, use 8 ounces of refrigerated sugar cookie dough. Slice dough according to package directions. Arrange dough slices in pan, starting on the outside edge and working your way into the middle. Press dough evenly onto the bottom of the pan. Bake as directed above.

Applesauce Filling

24 ounces	cream cheese
³/₄ cup	sugar
5 teaspoons	cornstarch
3	eggs
1	egg yolk
²/₃ cup	applesauce
¹/₃ cup	frozen apple juice concentrate, thawed
1 teaspoon	ground cinnamon
1 teaspoon	vanilla extract
¹/₄ teaspoon	ground nutmeg

In a large bowl combine cream cheese, sugar, and cornstarch. Beat with an electric mixer till smooth. Add eggs and egg yolk, one at a time, beating well after each addition. Beat in applesauce, apple juice concentrate, cinnamon, vanilla extract, and nutmeg. Pour the cream cheese mixture over the crust.

Bake at 350° for 15 minutes. Lower the temperature to 225° and bake for 1 hour and 10 minutes or till the center no longer looks wet or shiny. Remove the cake from the oven and run a knife around the inside edge of the pan. Turn the oven off; return the cake to the oven for an additional 30 minutes. Chill, uncovered, overnight.

Apple Glaze

¹/₂ cup	frozen apple juice concentrate, thawed
1 tablespoon	lemon juice
1 tablespoon	cornstarch
¹/₄ teaspoon	ground cinnamon
1 medium	apple, thinly sliced
2 tablespoons	lemon juice

In a small saucepan stir together apple juice concentrate, 1 tablespoon lemon juice, cornstarch, and cinnamon. Cook and stir till thickened and bubbly. Cook and stir 2 minutes more. Pour over cheesecake. Toss together apple slices and 2 tablespoons lemon juice. Arrange on top of cheesecake. Chill till serving time. Makes 12 to 18 slices.

Apricot Cheesecake

Fresh apricots and apricot nectar both contribute to the fruity taste of this cheesecake. Look for fresh apricots from late May to early August.

Vanilla Cookie Crust

11	vanilla sandwich cream cookies, crushed
3 tablespoons	butter or margarine, melted

In a small bowl stir together crushed cookies and melted butter or margarine till well combined. Press crumb mixture evenly onto the bottom of a greased 9-inch springform pan.

Apricot Filling

24 ounces	cream cheese
3/4 cup	sugar
5 teaspoons	cornstarch
3	eggs
1	egg yolk
1/2 cup	apricot nectar
1/4 cup	whipping cream
2 teaspoons	vanilla extract
4 medium	apricots; pitted, peeled and chopped
or	
1 cup	canned peeled whole apricots, drained and chopped

In a large bowl combine cream cheese, sugar, and cornstarch. Beat with an electric mixer till smooth. Add eggs and egg yolk, one at a time, beating well after each addition. Beat in apricot nectar, whipping cream, and vanilla extract. Stir in apricots. Pour the cream cheese mixture over the crust.

Bake at 375° for 15 minutes. Lower the temperature to 225° and bake for 1 hour and 10 minutes or till the center no longer looks wet or shiny. Remove the cake from the oven and run a knife around the inside edge of the pan. Turn the oven off; return the cake to the oven for an additional 1 hour. Chill, uncovered, overnight. Makes 12 to 18 slices.

Apricot Mousse Cheesecake

Apricot and almond grace this light-tasting cheesecake.

Vanilla Cookie Crust

11	vanilla sandwich cream cookies, crushed
3 tablespoons	chopped almonds
3 tablespoons	butter or margarine, melted

In a small bowl stir together crushed cookies and almonds. Stir in melted butter or margarine till well combined. Press crumb mixture evenly onto the bottom of a greased 9-inch springform pan.

Apricot Almond Filling

24 ounces	cream cheese
3/4 cup	sugar
5 teaspoons	cornstarch
3	eggs
1	egg yolk
1/2 cup	apricot nectar
2 tablespoons	amaretto
2 tablespoons	frozen orange juice concentrate, thawed
1 1/4 teaspoons	vanilla extract
1/2 cup	puréed apricots

In a large bowl combine cream cheese, sugar, and cornstarch. Beat with an electric mixer till smooth. Add eggs and egg yolk, one at a time, beating well after each addition. Beat in apricot nectar, amaretto, orange juice concentrate, and vanilla extract. Stir in puréed apricots. Pour the cream cheese mixture over the crust.

Bake at 350° for 15 minutes. Lower the temperature to 225° and bake for 1 hour and 10 minutes or till the center no longer looks wet or shiny. Remove the cake from the oven and run a knife around the inside edge of the pan. Turn the oven off; return the cake to the oven for an additional 1 hour. Chill, uncovered, overnight. Makes 12 to 18 slices.

Banana Cream Cheesecake

This easy-to-make cheesecake will remind you of a rich banana cream pie.

Vanilla Cookie Crust

| 11 | vanilla sandwich cream cookies, crushed |
| 3 tablespoons | butter or margarine, melted |

In a small bowl stir together crushed cookies and melted butter or margarine till well combined. Press crumb mixture evenly onto the bottom of a greased 9-inch springform pan.

Banana Cream Filling

24 ounces	cream cheese
$3/4$ cup	sugar
5 teaspoons	cornstarch
3	eggs
1	egg yolk
$2/3$ cup	puréed banana (2 small bananas)
$1/3$ cup	banana schnapps
$1^1/4$ teaspoons	vanilla extract

In a large bowl combine cream cheese, sugar, and cornstarch. Beat with an electric mixer till smooth. Add eggs and egg yolk, one at a time, beating well after each addition. Beat in puréed banana, banana schnapps, and vanilla extract. Pour the cream cheese mixture over the crust.

Bake at 350° for 15 minutes. Lower the temperature to 225° and bake for 1 hour and 10 minutes or till the center no longer looks wet or shiny. Remove the cake from the oven and run a knife around the inside edge of the pan. Turn the oven off; return the cake to the oven for an additional 30 minutes. Chill, uncovered, overnight. Makes 12 to 18 slices.

Bananas Foster Cheesecake

Bananas, rum, and brown sugar make this delightful cheesecake taste like the classic dessert.

Vanilla Cookie Crust

| 11 | vanilla sandwich cream cookies, crushed |
| 3 tablespoons | butter or margarine, melted |

In a small bowl stir together crushed cookies and melted butter or margarine till well combined. Press crumb mixture evenly onto the bottom of a greased 9-inch springform pan.

Bananas Foster Filling

24 ounces	cream cheese
$3/4$ cup	dark brown sugar
5 teaspoons	cornstarch
$3/4$ teaspoon	ground cinnamon
3	eggs
1	egg yolk
$2/3$ cup	puréed banana (2 small bananas)
3 tablespoons	banana schnapps
3 tablespoons	light rum
2 teaspoons	vanilla extract

In a large bowl combine cream cheese, brown sugar, cornstarch, and cinnamon. Beat with an electric mixer till smooth. Add eggs and egg yolk, one at a time, beating well after each addition. Beat in puréed banana, banana schnapps, rum, and vanilla extract. Pour the cream cheese mixture over the crust.

Bake at 350° for 15 minutes. Lower the temperature to 225° and bake for 1 hour and 10 minutes or till the center no longer looks wet or shiny. Remove the cake from the oven and run a knife around the inside edge of the pan. Turn the oven off; return the cake to the oven for an additional 30 minutes. Chill, uncovered, overnight.

Cherry Cheesecake

Cheesecake and cherries are a classic combination. Try this easy version when fresh bing cherries are in season.

Graham Cracker Crust

1¼ cups	graham cracker crumbs
3 tablespoons	sugar
¼ cup	butter or margarine, melted

In a small bowl stir together crumbs and sugar. Add melted butter or margarine. Stir till well combined. Press crumb mixture evenly onto the bottom of a greased 9-inch springform pan. Set aside.

Cherry Filling

24 ounces	cream cheese
¾ cup	sugar
⅔ cup	sour cream
5 teaspoons	cornstarch
4	eggs
1	egg yolk
¼ cup	cherry-flavored liqueur
2 teaspoons	vanilla extract
	Chopped pecans

In a large bowl combine cream cheese, sugar, sour cream, and cornstarch. Beat with an electric mixer till smooth. Add eggs and egg yolk, one at a time, beating well after each addition. Beat in liqueur and vanilla extract. Pour the cream cheese mixture over the crust.

Bake at 350° for 15 minutes. Lower the temperature to 225° and bake for 1 hour and 10 minutes or till the center no longer looks wet or shiny. Remove the cake from the oven and run a knife around the inside edge of the pan. Turn the oven off; return the cake to the oven for an additional 30 minutes. Chill, uncovered, overnight.

Bing Cherry Topping

3 tablespoons	sugar
1½ tablespoons	cornstarch
¼ cup	orange juice
1 pound	fresh bing cherries, pitted

In a small saucepan stir together sugar and cornstarch. Stir in orange juice. Stir in the cherries. Cook and stir over low heat about 5 minutes or till thickened and bubbly. Cook and stir 2 minutes more. Spread warm cherry mixture over the cake. Chill till serving time. Makes 12 to 18 slices.

Imperial Bing Cherry Cheesecake

This cherry-studded cheesecake is richer than most of the other cakes because it contains extra cream cheese and an additional egg. Slice it thin and enjoy!

Graham Cracker Crust

1¼ cups	graham cracker crumbs
3 tablespoons	sugar
¼ cup	butter or margarine, melted

In a small bowl stir together crumbs and sugar. Add melted butter or margarine. Stir till well combined. Press crumb mixture evenly onto the bottom of a greased 9-inch springform pan. Set aside.

Sweet Cherry Filling

32 ounces	cream cheese
¾ cup	sugar
3 tablespoons	cornstarch
4	eggs
1	egg yolk
½ cup	cherry-flavored liqueur
2 teaspoons	vanilla extract
1 8¾-ounce can	pitted dark sweet cherries, drained

In a large bowl combine cream cheese, sugar, and cornstarch. Beat with an electric mixer till smooth. Add eggs and egg yolk, one at a time, beating well after each addition. Beat in liqueur and vanilla extract. Stir in cherries. Pour the cream cheese mixture over the crust.

Bake at 325° for 15 minutes. Lower the temperature to 225° and bake for 1 hour and 30 minutes or till the center no longer looks wet or shiny. Remove the cake from the oven and run a knife around the inside edge of the pan. Chill, uncovered, overnight. Makes 18 slices.

Ambrosia Cheesecake

This luscious cheesecake is spectacular when you top it with fresh fruit and drizzle it with white and dark chocolate.

Coconut Crust

1²/₃ cups	flaked or freshly grated coconut
3 tablespoons	coarsely chopped almonds, toasted
3 tablespoons	butter or margarine, melted

In a small bowl stir together the coconut and chopped almonds. Add melted butter or margarine and stir till well combined. Press coconut mixture evenly onto the bottom of a 9-inch springform pan. Set aside.

Ambrosia Filling

24 ounces	cream cheese
5 teaspoons	cornstarch
³/₄ cup	sugar
¹/₂ cup	apricot nectar
¹/₄ cup	cream of coconut
3	eggs
1	egg yolk
1¹/₄ teaspoons	vanilla extract
1 8-ounce can	crushed pineapple, drained

In a large bowl combine cream cheese, sugar, and cornstarch. Beat with an electric mixer till smooth. Beat in apricot nectar and cream of coconut. Add eggs and egg yolk, one at a time, beating well after each addition. Beat in vanilla extract. Stir in drained pineapple. Pour cream cheese mixture over crust.

Bake at 350° for 15 minutes. Lower the temperature to 225° and bake for 1 hour and 10 minutes or until the center no longer looks wet or shiny. Remove the cake from the oven and run a knife around the inside edge of the pan. Turn the oven off; return the cake to the oven for an additional 1 hour. Chill, uncovered, overnight.

Fresh Fruit and Chocolate Topping

	Fresh fruit, sliced
	Walnuts
¹/₄ cup	white chocolate chips
1 tablespoon	light cream
1 teaspoon	cherry-flavored liqueur
¹/₄ cup	semisweet chocolate chips
1 tablespoon	light cream

Arrange fresh fruit and walnuts over cheesecake. Chill till serving time. Just before serving, in a small saucepan melt white chocolate chips, 1 tablespoon light cream, and liqueur over low heat, stirring constantly. Slice cheesecake and arrange on serving plates. Drizzle melted white chocolate mixture over cheesecake. In same saucepan, melt semisweet chocolate and 1 tablespoon light cream over low heat, stirring constantly. Drizzle over cheesecake. Makes 12 to 18 slices.

Blueberry Cheesecake

Make this a tradition at your house when fresh blueberries are in season from June through August.

Graham Cracker Crust

1¹/₄ cups	graham cracker crumbs
3 tablespoons	sugar
¹/₄ cup	butter or margarine, melted

In a small bowl stir together crumbs and sugar. Add melted butter or margarine. Stir till well combined. Press crumb mixture evenly onto the bottom of a greased 9-inch springform pan. Set aside.

Blueberry Filling

24 ounces	cream cheese
³/₄ cup	sugar
5 teaspoons	cornstarch
3	eggs
1	egg yolk
²/₃ cup	whipping cream
2 teaspoons	vanilla extract
1 teaspoon	finely shredded lemon peel
1 cup	fresh blueberries

In a large bowl combine cream cheese, sugar, and cornstarch. Beat with an electric mixer till smooth. Add eggs and egg yolk, one at a time, beating well after each addition. Stir in whipping cream, vanilla extract, and lemon peel. Fold in blueberries. Pour the cream cheese mixture over the crust.

Bake at 350° for 15 minutes. Lower the temperature to 225° and bake for 1 hour and 15 minutes or till the center no longer looks wet or shiny. Remove the cake from the oven and run a knife around the inside edge of the pan. Chill, uncovered, overnight. Makes 12 to 18 slices.

Blackberry Cheesecake

Blackberries and sweet blackberry wine give this cheese-cake its berry boost.

Vanilla Cookie Crust

11	vanilla sandwich cream cookies, crushed
3 tablespoons	chopped almonds, toasted
3 tablespoons	butter or margarine, melted

In a small bowl stir together crushed cookies and chopped almonds. Stir in melted butter or margarine till well combined. Press crumb mixture evenly onto the bottom of a greased 9-inch springform pan.

Blackberry Filling

24 ounces	cream cheese
3/4 cup	sugar
1/4 cup	sour cream
5 teaspoons	cornstarch
3/4 teaspoon	ground cinnamon
3	eggs
1	egg yolk
1/2 cup	sweet blackberry wine
2 teaspoons	almond extract
1 1/4 teaspoons	vanilla extract
2/3 cup	fresh or frozen and thawed blackberries, drained
1/4 cup	chopped almonds, toasted

In a large bowl combine cream cheese, sugar, sour cream, cornstarch, and cinnamon. Beat with an electric mixer till smooth. Add eggs and egg yolk, one at a time, beating well after each addition. Beat in sweet blackberry wine, almond extract, and vanilla extract. Stir in blackberries and almonds. Pour the cream cheese mixture over the crust.

Bake at 350° for 15 minutes. Lower the temperature to 225° and bake for 1 hour and 10 minutes or till the center no longer looks wet or shiny. Remove the cake from the oven and run a knife around the inside edge of the pan. Chill, uncovered, overnight. Makes 12 to 18 slices.

Cherry Almond Cheesecake

Be sure to toast the almonds for a nuttier flavor and crunchier texture.

Graham Cracker Crust

1 1/4 cups	graham cracker crumbs
3 tablespoons	sugar
1/4 teaspoon	ground cinnamon
1/4 cup	butter or margarine, melted

In a small bowl stir together crumbs, sugar, and cinnamon. Add melted butter or margarine. Stir till well combined. Press crumb mixture evenly onto the bottom of a greased 9-inch springform pan. Set aside.

Cherry Almond Filling

18 ounces	fresh bing cherries, pitted
2/3 cup	sugar
1 1/2 tablespoons	cornstarch
24 ounces	cream cheese
3/4 cup	sugar
5 teaspoons	cornstarch
3	eggs
1	egg yolk
4 teaspoons	lemon juice
2 teaspoons	almond extract
1 teaspoon	vanilla extract
1/3 cup	chopped almonds, toasted

In a small saucepan stir together cherries and 2/3 cup sugar. Let stand 30 minutes. Stir in 1 1/2 tablespoons cornstarch. Cook and stir till thickened. Set aside.

In a large bowl combine cream cheese, 3/4 cup sugar, and 5 teaspoons cornstarch. Beat with an electric mixer till smooth. Add eggs and egg yolk, one at a time, beating well after each addition. Beat in lemon juice, almond extract, and vanilla extract. Stir in almonds.

Pour half of the batter over the crust. Spoon half of the cherry mixture over the batter. Top with remaining batter. Spoon remaining cherry mixture over the top.

Bake at 400° for 15 minutes. Lower the temperature to 225° and bake for 1 hour and 15 minutes or till the center no longer looks wet or shiny. Remove the cake from the oven and run a knife around the inside edge of the pan. Turn the oven off; return the cake to the oven for an additional 1 hour. Chill, uncovered, overnight.

Easy Cherry Topping

1 cup	cherry preserves
1 tablespoon	orange-flavored liqueur
1/3 cup	chopped almonds, toasted

In a small saucepan heat cherry preserves over low heat. Remove from heat and stir in liqueur. Spoon over cheesecake just before serving. Sprinkle with almonds. Makes 12 to 18 slices.

Chocolate Cherry Almond Cheesecake

This fun-to-make cheesecake sports a chocolate crust and a swirled chocolate and cherry filling.

Chocolate Cookie Crust

11	chocolate sandwich cream cookies, crushed
3 tablespoons	chopped almonds, toasted
3 tablespoons	butter or margarine, melted

In a small bowl stir together crushed cookies and almonds. Stir in melted butter or margarine till well combined. Press crumb mixture evenly onto the bottom of a greased 9-inch springform pan.

Chocolate Cherry Almond Filling

24 ounces	cream cheese
2/3 cup	sugar
5 teaspoons	cornstarch
3	eggs
1	egg yolk
1 1/4 teaspoons	vanilla extract
5 teaspoons	unsweetened cocoa powder
2 1/2 tablespoons	sugar
1/2 cup	cherry schnapps
1 1/2 teaspoons	almond extract
2/3 cup	bing cherries, pitted, chopped, and drained

In a large bowl combine cream cheese, 2/3 cup sugar, and cornstarch. Beat with an electric mixer till smooth. Add eggs and egg yolk, one at a time, beating well after each addition. Beat in vanilla extract.

Remove 3/4 cup of the mixture and put into a small bowl; stir in cocoa powder and 2 1/2 tablespoons sugar. Set aside. Stir cherry schnapps and almond extract into the remaining cream cheese mixture. Fold in cherries.

Pour half of the cherry mixture over the crust. Spoon 2/3 cup of the cocoa mixture over the cherry mixture. Pour the remaining cherry mixture over the cocoa mixture. Top with remaining cocoa mixture. Without disturbing the crust, swirl the blade of a knife through the cake to create a marbling effect.

Bake at 325° for 15 minutes. Lower the temperature to 225° and bake for 1 hour and 10 minutes or till the center no longer looks wet or shiny. Remove the cake from the oven and run a knife around the inside edge of the pan. Turn the oven off; return the cake to the oven for an additional 1 hour. Chill, uncovered, overnight. Makes 12 to 18 slices.

Banana Split Cheesecake

This extraordinary cheesecake is the ideal choice for a festive birthday celebration. You'll have fun decorating this colorful dessert.

Chocolate Cookie Crust

1³/₄ cups	finely crushed chocolate wafers
3 tablespoons	sugar
¹/₂ cup	butter or margarine, melted

In a small bowl stir together crushed wafers and sugar. Add melted butter or margarine. Stir till well combined. Press crumb mixture evenly onto the bottom and up the sides of a greased 9-inch springform pan. Set aside.

Banana Split Filling

24 ounces	cream cheese
³/₄ cup	sugar
5 teaspoons	cornstarch
3	eggs
1	egg yolk
²/₃ cup	puréed banana (2 small bananas)
¹/₂ cup	banana schnapps
2 teaspoons	vanilla extract

In a large bowl combine cream cheese, sugar, and cornstarch. Beat with an electric mixer till smooth. Add eggs and egg yolk, one at a time, beating well after each addition. Beat in puréed banana, banana schnapps, and vanilla extract. Pour the cream cheese mixture over the crust.

Bake at 350° for 15 minutes. Lower the temperature to 225° and bake for 1 hour and 10 minutes or till the center no longer looks wet or shiny. Remove the cake from the oven and run a knife around the inside edge of the pan. Turn the oven off; return the cake to the oven for an additional 30 minutes. Chill, uncovered, overnight.

Pineapple, Strawberry, and Chocolate Topping

Fresh pineapple chunks
Fresh strawberries
Chocolate ice cream topping, heated
Whipped cream
Chopped nuts

Just before serving, garnish cheesecake with pineapple and strawberries. Drizzle with warm ice cream topping. Dollop with whipped cream and sprinkle with nuts. Makes 12 to 18 slices.

Creamy Lemon Cheesecake

Graham Cracker Crust

1¹/₄ cups	graham cracker crumbs
3 tablespoons	sugar
¹/₄ cup	butter or margarine, melted

In a small bowl stir together crumbs and sugar. Add melted butter or margarine. Stir till well combined. Press crumb mixture evenly onto the bottom of a greased 9-inch springform pan. Set aside.

Creamy Lemon Filling

24 ounces	cream cheese
³/₄ cup	sugar
5 teaspoons	cornstarch
3	eggs
1	egg yolk
¹/₂ cup	frozen lemonade concentrate, thawed
¹/₄ cup	sour cream
2 tablespoons	lemon juice
2 teaspoons	vanilla extract
1 teaspoon	finely shredded lemon peel
	Fresh lemon slices

In a large bowl combine cream cheese, sugar, and cornstarch. Beat with an electric mixer till smooth. Add eggs and egg yolk, one at a time, beating well after each addition. Beat in lemonade concentrate, sour cream, lemon juice, vanilla extract, and lemon peel. Pour the cream cheese mixture over the crust.

Bake at 350° for 15 minutes. Lower the temperature to 200° and bake for 1 hour and 10 minutes or till the center no longer looks wet or shiny. Remove the cake from the oven and run a knife around the inside edge of the pan. Turn the oven off; return the cake to the oven for an additional 1 hour. Chill, uncovered, overnight.

Lemon Sour Cream Topping

1 cup	sour cream
1 tablespoon	sugar
1 tablespoon	lemon juice
2 teaspoons	finely shredded lemon peel
	Fresh lemon slices

In a small bowl stir together sour cream, sugar, lemon juice, and lemon peel. Spread over cheesecake. Garnish with lemon slices. Chill till serving time. Makes 12 to 18 slices.

Creamy Orange Swirl Cheesecake

This citrus cheesecake tastes like a cross between orange sherbet and an orange julius beverage.

Vanilla Cookie Crust

11	vanilla sandwich cream cookies, crushed
3 tablespoons	butter or margarine, melted

In a small bowl stir together crushed cookies and melted butter or margarine till well combined. Press crumb mixture evenly onto the bottom of a greased 9-inch springform pan.

Orange Swirl Filling

24 ounces	cream cheese
3/4 cup	sugar
2 1/2 tablespoons	whipping cream
5 teaspoons	cornstarch
4	eggs
1	egg yolk
1/3 cup	frozen orange juice concentrate, thawed
1 teaspoon	finely shredded orange peel
1/3 cup	vanilla-flavored liqueur
1 1/4 teaspoons	vanilla extract

In a large bowl combine cream cheese, sugar, whipping cream, and cornstarch. Beat with an electric mixer till smooth. Add eggs and egg yolk, one at a time, beating well after each addition.

Remove half of the mixture and put into a small bowl; stir in orange juice concentrate and orange peel. Set aside. Stir liqueur and vanilla extract into the remaining cream cheese mixture.

Pour the orange mixture over the crust. Top with the vanilla mixture. Without disturbing the crust, swirl the blade of a knife through the cake to create a marbling effect.

Bake at 350° for 15 minutes. Lower the temperature to 225° and bake for 1 hour and 10 minutes or till the center no longer looks wet or shiny. Remove the cake from the oven and run a knife around the inside edge of the pan. Chill, uncovered, overnight.

Orange Sour Cream Topping

1 cup	sour cream
1 tablespoon	sugar
1 tablespoon	orange juice
1/2 teaspoon	finely shredded orange peel
	Fresh orange slices

In a small bowl stir together sour cream, sugar, orange juice, and orange peel. Spread over cheesecake. Garnish with orange slices. Chill till serving time. Makes 12 to 18 slices.

Key Lime Cheesecake

Look for bottled key lime juice on your grocer's shelves.

Homemade Cookie Crust

3/4 cup	flour
2 1/2 tablespoons	sugar
1	egg, lightly beaten
1/4 cup	butter or margarine, softened
1/2 teaspoon	vanilla extract

In a medium bowl stir together flour and sugar. Add egg, butter or margarine, and vanilla extract. Beat with an electric mixer till well combined. With generously greased fingers, press the dough evenly onto the bottom of a greased 9-inch springform pan.

Bake at 350° for 12 to 15 minutes or till lightly browned. Remove from oven and set aside.

Refrigerated Cookie Dough Crust: In place of Homemade Cookie Crust, use 8 ounces of refrigerated sugar cookie dough. Slice dough according to package directions. Arrange dough slices in pan, starting on the outside edge and working your way into the middle. Press dough evenly onto the bottom of the pan. Bake as directed above.

Key Lime Filling

24 ounces	cream cheese
3/4 cup	sugar
5 tablespoons	sour cream
5 teaspoons	flour
4	eggs
1	egg yolk
1/2 cup	frozen limeade concentrate, thawed
1/4 cup	lime juice
1 teaspoon	vanilla extract
	Green food coloring (optional)

In a large bowl combine cream cheese, sugar, sour cream, and flour. Beat with an electric mixer till smooth. Add eggs and egg yolk, one at a time, beating well after each addition. Beat in limeade concentrate, lime juice, and vanilla extract. Stir in green food coloring, if desired. Pour the cream cheese mixture over the crust.

Bake at 350° for 15 minutes. Lower the temperature to 200° and bake for 1 hour and 10 minutes or till the center no longer looks wet or shiny. Remove the cake from the oven and run a knife around the inside edge of the pan.

Honey Lime Glaze

1/2 cup	frozen limeade concentrate, thawed
4 teaspoons	lime juice
1 tablespoon	cornstarch
1 tablespoon	honey
1 teaspoon	finely shredded lime peel
	Fresh lime slices

In a small saucepan stir together limeade concentrate, lime juice, cornstarch, honey, and lime peel. Cook and stir till thickened and bubbly. Cook and stir 2 minutes more. Pour over cheesecake. Garnish with lime slices. Chill till serving time. Makes 12 to 18 slices.

Lemon Drop Cheesecake

Serve this light-tasting cheesecake on a sultry summer day.

Graham Cracker Crust

1 1/4 cups	graham cracker crumbs
3 tablespoons	sugar
1/4 cup	butter or margarine, melted

In a small bowl stir together crumbs and sugar. Add melted butter or margarine. Stir till well combined. Press crumb mixture evenly onto the bottom of a greased 9-inch springform pan. Set aside.

Lemon Drop Filling

24 ounces	cream cheese
3/4 cup	sugar
1/2 cup	sour cream
5 teaspoons	cornstarch
3	eggs
1	egg yolk
3 tablespoons	frozen lemonade concentrate, thawed
2 teaspoons	vanilla extract
	Yellow food coloring (optional)

In a large bowl combine cream cheese, sugar, sour cream, and cornstarch. Beat with an electric mixer till smooth. Add eggs and egg yolk, one at a time, beating well after each addition. Beat in lemonade concentrate and vanilla extract. Stir in food coloring, if desired. Pour the cream cheese mixture over the crust.

Bake at 350° for 15 minutes. Lower the temperature to 200° and bake for 1 hour and 10 minutes or till the center no longer looks wet or shiny. Remove the cake from the oven and run a knife around the inside edge of the pan. Chill, uncovered, overnight.

Easy Lemon Topping

1 cup	whipping cream
1 tablespoon	sugar
1 teaspoon	finely shredded lemon peel
	Small lemon wedges

In a small bowl beat whipping cream, sugar, and lemon peel with an electric mixer till stiff peaks form. Pipe whipped cream mixture around the edge of the cheesecake. Garnish with lemon wedges. Chill till serving time. Makes 12 to 18 slices.

Limon Cheesecake

As the name implies, this cheesecake is a refreshing blend of lime juice and lemon juice.

Graham Cracker Crust

1¼ cups	graham cracker crumbs
3 tablespoons	sugar
¼ cup	butter or margarine, melted

In a small bowl stir together crumbs and sugar. Add melted butter or margarine. Stir till well combined. Press crumb mixture evenly onto the bottom of a greased 9-inch springform pan. Set aside.

Limon Filling

24 ounces	cream cheese
¾ cup	sugar
¼ cup	sour cream
5 teaspoons	cornstarch
4	eggs
1	egg yolk
¼ cup	frozen limeade concentrate, thawed
¼ cup	frozen lemonade concentrate, thawed
1 tablespoon	lime juice
1 tablespoon	lemon juice
1 teaspoon	finely shredded lime peel
1 teaspoon	finely shredded lemon peel
1 teaspoon	vanilla extract

In a large bowl combine cream cheese, sugar, sour cream, and cornstarch. Beat with an electric mixer till smooth. Add eggs and egg yolk, one at a time, beating well after each addition. Beat in limeade concentrate, lemonade concentrate, lime juice, lemon juice, lime peel, lemon peel, and vanilla extract. Pour the cream cheese mixture over the crust.

Bake at 350° for 15 minutes. Lower the temperature to 200° and bake for 1 hour and 10 minutes or till the center no longer looks wet or shiny. Remove the cake from the oven and run a knife around the inside edge of the pan. Chill, uncovered, overnight.

Easy Limon Topping

1 cup	whipping cream
1 tablespoon	sugar
1 teaspoon	finely shredded lime peel
1 teaspoon	finely shredded lemon peel
	Small lime wedges
	Small lemon wedges

In a small bowl beat whipping cream, sugar, lime peel, and lemon peel with an electric mixer till stiff peaks form. Pipe whipped cream mixture around the edge of the cheesecake. Garnish with lime and lemon wedges. Chill till serving time. Makes 12 to 18 slices.

New England Apple Cheesecake

You'll savor this unique blend of applesauce, apple juice, cheddar cheese, walnuts, and apple pie spices.

Cheddar Walnut Cookie Crust

¾ cup	flour
2½ tablespoons	sugar
½ teaspoon	ground cinnamon
1	egg, lightly beaten
¼ cup	butter or margarine, softened
½ cup	shredded cheddar cheese
2 tablespoons	chopped walnuts

In a medium bowl stir together flour, sugar, and cinnamon. Add egg and butter or margarine. Beat with an electric mixer till well combined. Stir in cheddar cheese and walnuts. With generously greased fingers, press the dough evenly onto the bottom of a greased 9-inch springform pan.

Bake at 350° for 15 to 20 minutes or till lightly browned. Remove from oven and set aside.

Apple Cheese Filling

18 ounces	cream cheese
2/3 cup	light brown sugar
5 teaspoons	cornstarch
4	eggs
2/3 cup	applesauce
1/3 cup	frozen apple juice concentrate, thawed
2 teaspoons	ground cinnamon
2 teaspoons	vanilla extract
1 teaspoon	ground nutmeg
1/4 teaspoon	ground cloves
1 cup	shredded cheddar cheese
1/4 cup	chopped walnuts

In a large bowl combine cream cheese, brown sugar, and cornstarch. Beat with an electric mixer till smooth. Add eggs, one at a time, beating well after each addition. Beat in applesauce, apple juice concentrate, cinnamon, vanilla extract, nutmeg, and cloves. Stir in cheese and walnuts. Pour the cream cheese mixture over the crust.

Bake at 350° for 15 minutes. Lower the temperature to 225° and bake for 1 hour and 10 minutes or till the center no longer looks wet or shiny. Remove the cake from the oven and run a knife around the inside edge of the pan. Turn the oven off; return the cake to the oven for an additional 1 hour. Chill, uncovered, overnight.

Apple Walnut Topping

1/3 cup	frozen apple juice concentrate, thawed
1 tablespoon	light brown sugar
1 tablespoon	cornstarch
1/4 teaspoon	ground cinnamon
2 tablespoons	port wine
1/4 cup	chopped walnuts

In a small saucepan stir together apple juice concentrate, brown sugar, cornstarch, and cinnamon. Cook and stir till thickened and bubbly. Cook and stir 2 minutes more. Stir in port. Pour over cheesecake. Sprinkle with walnuts. Chill till serving time. Makes 12 to 18 slices.

Peaches 'n' Cream Cheesecake

This rich cheesecake is bursting with fresh peaches. Choose peaches that are plump, somewhat firm, and have a creamy yellow color with a good pink blush.

Graham Cracker Crust

1 1/4 cups	graham cracker crumbs
3 tablespoons	sugar
1/4 teaspoon	ground cinnamon
1/4 cup	butter or margarine, melted

In a small bowl stir together crumbs, sugar, and cinnamon. Add melted butter or margarine. Stir till well combined. Press crumb mixture evenly onto the bottom of a greased 9-inch springform pan. Set aside.

Peach Filling

24 ounces	cream cheese
3/4 cup	sugar
5 teaspoons	cornstarch
4	eggs
1	egg yolk
1 teaspoon	vanilla extract
1 teaspoon	lemon juice
2/3 cup	whipping cream
1 1/3 cups	peeled and finely chopped peaches

In a large bowl combine cream cheese, sugar, and cornstarch. Beat with an electric mixer till smooth. Add eggs and egg yolk, one at a time, beating well after each addition. Beat in vanilla extract and lemon juice. Stir in whipping cream. Fold in peaches. Pour the cream cheese mixture over the crust.

Bake at 350° for 10 minutes. Lower the temperature to 225° and bake for 1 hour and 10 minutes or till the center no longer looks wet or shiny. Remove the cake from the oven and run a knife around the inside edge of the pan. Turn the oven off; return the cake to the oven for an additional 1 hour. Chill, uncovered, overnight.

Fresh Peach Topping

2 medium	peaches, sliced
1 tablespoon	lemon juice
1 cup	peach preserves

Toss together peaches and lemon juice. Arrange on top of the cheesecake. Chill till serving time. Just before serving, in a small saucepan heat peach preserves. Drizzle warm preserves over cheesecake. Makes 12 to 18 slices.

Pear Elegance Cheesecake

A chocolate cookie crust, fresh pear filling, and easy pear glaze give this cheesecake an air of elegance.

Chocolate Cookie Crust

11	chocolate sandwich cream cookies, crushed
3 tablespoons	butter or margarine, melted

In a small bowl stir together crushed cookies and melted butter or margarine till well combined. Press crumb mixture evenly onto the bottom of a greased 9-inch springform pan.

Pear Filling

24 ounces	cream cheese
2/3 cup	sugar
5 teaspoons	cornstarch
3	eggs
1	egg yolk
2/3 cup	puréed pear (1 medium pear)
1/2 cup	pear schnapps
1 teaspoon	finely shredded lemon or orange peel
1 teaspoon	vanilla extract

In a large bowl combine cream cheese, sugar, and cornstarch. Beat with an electric mixer till smooth. Add eggs and egg yolk, one at a time, beating well after each addition. Beat in puréed pear, pear schnapps, lemon or orange peel, and vanilla extract. Pour the cream cheese mixture over the crust.

Bake at 350° for 15 minutes. Lower the temperature to 225° and bake for 1 hour and 10 minutes or till the center no longer looks wet or shiny. Remove the cake from the oven and run a knife around the inside edge of the pan. Turn the oven off; return the cake to the oven for an additional 30 minutes. Chill, uncovered, overnight.

Pear Glaze

1/2 cup	pear preserves
1/2 cup	orange marmalade
2 teaspoons	lemon juice
1/2 medium	pear, sliced

In a small saucepan stir together pear preserves and orange marmalade. Cook and stir till heated through. Pour over cheesecake. Dip pear slices in lemon juice. Arrange pear slices over cheesecake. Chill till serving time. Makes 12 to 18 slices.

Peach Pecan Cheesecake

This cheesecake combines fresh peaches and crunchy pecans for a scrumptious merger.

Vanilla Cookie Crust

11	vanilla sandwich cream cookies, crushed
3 tablespoons	chopped pecans
3 tablespoons	butter or margarine, melted

In a small bowl stir together crushed cookies and pecans. Stir in melted butter or margarine till well combined. Press crumb mixture evenly onto the bottom of a greased 9-inch springform pan.

Peach Pecan Filling

24 ounces	cream cheese
3/4 cup	dark brown sugar
5 teaspoons	cornstarch
4	eggs
1	egg yolk
1/3 cup	peach schnapps
3 tablespoons	whipping cream
1 teaspoon	vanilla extract
1 1/4 cup	peeled and finely chopped peaches
1/4 cup	chopped pecans

In a large bowl combine cream cheese, brown sugar, and cornstarch. Beat with an electric mixer till smooth. Add eggs and egg yolk, one at a time, beating well after each addition. Beat in peach schnapps, whipping cream, and vanilla extract. Stir in peaches and pecans. Pour the cream cheese mixture over the crust.

Bake at 350° for 15 minutes. Lower the temperature to 225° and bake for 1 hour and 10 minutes or till the center no longer looks wet or shiny. Remove the cake from the oven and run a knife around the inside edge of the pan. Turn the oven off; return the cake to the oven for an additional 1 hour. Chill, uncovered, overnight. Makes 12 to 18 slices.

Fresh Pineapple Cheesecake

Look for cored and peeled pineapple in your grocer's produce section.

Vanilla Cookie Crust

| 11 | vanilla sandwich cream cookies, crushed |
| 3 tablespoons | butter or margarine, melted |

In a small bowl stir together crushed cookies and melted butter or margarine till well combined. Press crumb mixture evenly onto the bottom of a greased 9-inch springform pan.

Pineapple Filling

27 ounces	cream cheese
3/4 cup	sugar
5 teaspoons	cornstarch
3	eggs
1	egg yolk
1/2 cup	frozen pineapple juice concentrate, thawed
1 teaspoon	finely shredded lemon peel
1 teaspoon	vanilla extract
1 cup	pineapple; cored, peeled, and finely chopped

In a large bowl combine cream cheese, sugar, and cornstarch. Beat with an electric mixer till smooth. Add eggs and egg yolk, one at a time, beating well after each addition. Beat in pineapple juice concentrate, lemon peel, and vanilla extract. Stir in pineapple. Pour the cream cheese mixture over the crust.

Bake at 350° for 15 minutes. Lower the temperature to 225° and bake for 1 hour and 10 minutes or till the center no longer looks wet or shiny. Remove the cake from the oven and run a knife around the inside edge of the pan. Turn the oven off; return the cake to the oven for an additional 1 hour. Chill, uncovered, overnight. Makes 12 to 18 slices.

Strawberry Chocolate Cheesecake

To make the chocolate-covered strawberries for the topping, simply melt 1/2 cup semisweet chocolate chips over low heat, stirring constantly. Spoon chocolate over 12 whole strawberries. Place on a baking sheet lined with waxed paper and chill till chocolate hardens.

Chocolate Cookie Crust

| 11 | chocolate sandwich cream cookies, crushed |
| 3 tablespoons | butter or margarine, melted |

In a small bowl stir together crushed cookies and melted butter or margarine till well combined. Press crumb mixture evenly onto the bottom of a greased 9-inch springform pan.

Strawberry Chocolate Filling

24 ounces	cream cheese
3/4 cup	sugar
5 teaspoons	cornstarch
3	eggs
1	egg yolk
1 1/4 teaspoons	vanilla extract
5 teaspoons	unsweetened cocoa powder
2 1/2 tablespoons	sugar
1/2 cup	strawberry schnapps
2/3 cup	sliced strawberries

In a large bowl combine cream cheese, 3/4 cup sugar, and cornstarch. Beat with an electric mixer till smooth. Add eggs and egg yolk, one at a time, beating well after each addition. Beat in vanilla extract.

Remove 3/4 cup of the mixture and put into a small bowl; stir in cocoa powder and 2 1/2 tablespoons sugar. Set aside. Stir strawberry schnapps into the remaining cream cheese mixture. Fold in strawberries.

Pour half of the strawberry mixture over the crust. Spoon half of the cocoa mixture over the strawberry mixture. Pour the remaining strawberry mixture over the cocoa mixture. Top with remaining cocoa mixture. Without disturbing the crust, swirl the blade of a knife through the cake to create a marbling effect.

Bake at 325° for 15 minutes. Lower the temperature to 225° and bake for 1 hour and 10 minutes or till the center no longer looks wet or shiny. Remove the cake from the oven and run a knife around the inside edge of the pan. Turn the oven off; return the cake to the oven for an additional 1 hour. Chill, uncovered, overnight.

Easy Whipped Cream Topping

1 cup	whipping cream
1 tablespoon	sugar
	Chocolate-dipped strawberries

In a small bowl beat whipping cream and sugar with an electric mixer till stiff peaks form. Pipe whipped cream mixture around the edge of the cheesecake. Garnish with chocolate-dipped strawberries. Chill till serving time. Makes 12 to 18 slices.

Raspberry Almond Cheesecake

Fresh raspberries are at their peak from July through September. For the best results, use them within 24 hours after you buy them.

Vanilla Cookie Crust

11	vanilla sandwich cream cookies, crushed
3 tablespoons	chopped almonds, toasted
3 tablespoons	butter or margarine, melted

In a small bowl stir together crushed cookies and almonds. Stir in melted butter or margarine till well combined. Press crumb mixture evenly onto the bottom of a greased 9-inch springform pan.

Raspberry Almond Filling

24 ounces	cream cheese
3/4 cup	sugar
1/4 cup	sour cream
5 teaspoons	cornstarch
4	eggs
1	egg yolk
1/2 cup	raspberry schnapps
1 1/2 teaspoons	almond extract
1 teaspoon	vanilla extract
1/2 teaspoon	ground cinnamon
2/3 cup	fresh raspberries
1/4 cup	chopped almonds, toasted

In a large bowl combine cream cheese, sugar, sour cream, and cornstarch. Beat with an electric mixer till smooth. Add eggs and egg yolk, one at a time, beating well after each addition. Beat in raspberry schnapps, almond extract, vanilla extract, and cinnamon. Stir in raspberries and almonds. Pour the cream cheese mixture over the crust.

Bake at 350° for 15 minutes. Lower the temperature to 225° and bake for 1 hour and 10 minutes or till the center no longer looks wet or shiny. Remove the cake from the oven and run a knife around the inside edge of the pan. Chill, uncovered, overnight.

Easy Raspberry Topping

1 cup	whipping cream
1 tablespoon	sugar
	Fresh raspberries

In a small bowl beat whipping cream and sugar with an electric mixer till stiff peaks form. Pipe whipped cream mixture around the edge of the cheesecake. Garnish with raspberries. Chill till serving time. Makes 12 to 18 slices.

Strawberry Cheesecake

America's favorite berry tastes great in this easy cheesecake. Buy enough fresh berries for the filling and the topping.

Graham Cracker Crust

1¼ cups	graham cracker crumbs
3 tablespoons	sugar
¼ cup	butter or margarine, melted

In a small bowl stir together crumbs and sugar. Add melted butter or margarine. Stir till well combined. Press crumb mixture evenly onto the bottom of a greased 9-inch springform pan. Set aside.

Strawberry Filling

24 ounces	cream cheese
¾ cup	sugar
5 teaspoons	cornstarch
4	eggs
1	egg yolk
1 tablespoon	lemon juice
1 teaspoon	vanilla extract
1¼ cups	sliced strawberries

In a large bowl combine cream cheese, sugar, and cornstarch. Beat with an electric mixer till smooth. Add eggs and egg yolk, one at a time, beating well after each addition. Beat in lemon juice and vanilla extract. Carefully stir in strawberries. Pour the cream cheese mixture over the crust.

Bake at 350° for 15 minutes. Lower the temperature to 225° and bake for 1 hour and 10 minutes or till the center no longer looks wet or shiny. Remove the cake from the oven and run a knife around the inside edge of the pan. Turn the oven off; return the cake to the oven for an additional 30 minutes. Chill, uncovered, overnight.

Creamy White Topping

½ cup	shortening
¾ teaspoon	vanilla extract
2½ cups	sifted powdered sugar
1½ to 2 tablespoons	milk
	Fresh strawberries

In a medium bowl beat shortening and vanilla extract with an electric mixer till smooth. Slowly add half of the powdered sugar, beating well. Add 1 tablespoon milk. Gradually beat in remaining powdered sugar. Add enough remaining milk to make of spreading consistency. Spread over cheesecake. Garnish with strawberries. Chill till serving time. Makes 12 to 18 slices.

Tangerine Cheesecake

A tangerine is a small, bright orange fruit that resembles an orange. It has loose skin and a sweet pulp. Look for fresh tangerines from November to May and choose ones that are heavy and firm with fairly tight skin.

Vanilla Cookie Crust

11	vanilla sandwich cream cookies, crushed
3 tablespoons	butter or margarine, melted

In a small bowl stir together crushed cookies and melted butter or margarine till well combined. Press crumb mixture evenly onto the bottom of a greased 9-inch springform pan.

Tangerine Filling

24 ounces	cream cheese
⅔ cup	sugar
5 teaspoons	cornstarch
1 tablespoon	sour cream
3	eggs
1	egg yolk
⅔ cup	frozen tangerine or orange juice concentrate, thawed
1 teaspoon	finely shredded orange peel
1 teaspoon	vanilla extract
1 medium	tangerine; peeled, seeded, and separated into segments

In a large bowl combine cream cheese, sugar, cornstarch, and sour cream. Beat with an electric mixer till smooth. Add eggs and egg yolk, one at a time, beating well after each addition. Beat in tangerine or orange juice concentrate, orange peel, and vanilla extract. Pour the cream cheese mixture over the crust. Arrange tangerine segments over the cream cheese mixture.

Bake at 350° for 15 minutes. Lower the temperature to 225° and bake for 1 hour and 10 minutes or till the center no longer looks wet or shiny. Remove the cake from the oven and run a knife around the inside edge of the pan. Chill, uncovered, overnight. Makes 12 to 18 slices.

Raspberry Chocolate Cheesecake

Chocolate Cookie Crust

11	milk chocolate sandwich cream cookies, crushed
3 tablespoons	chopped almonds, toasted
3 tablespoons	butter or margarine, melted

In a small bowl stir together crushed cookies and almonds. Stir in melted butter or margarine till well combined. Press crumb mixture evenly onto the bottom of a greased 9-inch springform pan.

Raspberry Filling

24 ounces	cream cheese
¾ cup	sugar
¼ cup	sour cream
5 teaspoons	cornstarch
3	eggs
1	egg yolk
⅓ cup	raspberry schnapps
1 teaspoon	finely shredded lemon peel
1 teaspoon	vanilla extract
1 teaspoon	almond extract
½ teaspoon	ground cinnamon
½ cup	fresh raspberries

In a large bowl combine cream cheese, sugar, sour cream, and cornstarch. Beat with an electric mixer till smooth. Add eggs and egg yolk, one at a time, beating well after each addition. Beat in raspberry schnapps, lemon peel, vanilla extract, almond extract, and cinnamon. Stir in raspberries. Pour the cream cheese mixture over the crust.

Bake at 350° for 15 minutes. Lower the temperature to 225° and bake for 1 hour and 10 minutes or till the center no longer looks wet or shiny. Remove the cake from the oven and run a knife around the inside edge of the pan. Turn the oven off; return the cake to the oven for an additional 30 minutes. Chill, uncovered, overnight.

Chocolate Raspberry Topping

3 ounces	semisweet chocolate, coarsely chopped
¼ cup	raspberry preserves, jelly, or jam Fresh raspberries

In a small saucepan melt chocolate over low heat, stirring constantly. Stir in raspberry preserves, jelly, or jam. Spread the warm chocolate mixture over the cake. Garnish with fresh raspberries. Chill till serving time. Makes 12 to 18 slices.

Cranberry Orange Cheesecake

This beautiful cheesecake is great for the holidays but can be made all year round. Simply stock up on fresh cranberries in November and store them in your freezer.

Vanilla Wafer Crust

1¾ cups	crushed vanilla wafers
3 tablespoons	chopped walnuts
¼ cup	butter or margarine, melted

In a small bowl stir together crushed wafers and walnuts. Add melted butter or margarine. Stir till well combined. Press crumb mixture evenly onto the bottom of a greased 9-inch springform pan. Set aside.

Cranberry Orange Filling

24 ounces	cream cheese
¾ cup	sugar
5 teaspoons	cornstarch
3	eggs
1	egg yolk
½ cup	frozen cranberry juice cocktail concentrate, thawed
1 teaspoon	finely shredded orange peel
1 teaspoon	vanilla extract
1 cup	fresh cranberries, finely chopped
⅓ cup	finely chopped walnuts

In a large bowl combine cream cheese, sugar, and cornstarch. Beat with an electric mixer till smooth. Add eggs and egg yolk, one at a time, beating well after each addition. Beat in cranberry juice cocktail, orange peel, and vanilla extract. Stir in cranberries and walnuts. Pour the cream cheese mixture over the crust.

Bake at 350° for 15 minutes. Lower the temperature to 225° and bake for 1 hour and 10 minutes or till the center no longer looks wet or shiny. Remove the cake from the oven and run a knife around the inside edge of the pan. Chill, uncovered, overnight.

Cranberry Orange Glaze

½ cup	frozen cranberry juice cocktail concentrate, thawed
⅓ cup	orange marmalade
2 teaspoons	lemon juice

In a small saucepan stir together cranberry juice concentrate, orange marmalade, and lemon juice. Cook and stir till thickened and bubbly. Cook and stir 2 minutes more. Pour over cheesecake. Chill till serving time. Makes 12 to 18 slices.

Mint Cheesecakes

Peppermint Chip Cheesecake

Romance your guests by making individual heart-shaped cheesecakes. Simply use 4-inch heart-shaped tart pans and bake at 225° for 35 to 45 minutes.

Chocolate Mint Cookie Crust

11	chocolate mint or chocolate sandwich cream cookies, crushed
3 tablespoons	butter or margarine, melted

In a small bowl stir together crushed cookies and melted butter or margarine till well combined. Press crumb mixture evenly onto the bottom of a greased 9-inch springform pan.

Peppermint Chip Filling

24 ounces	cream cheese
³/₄ cup	sugar
5 teaspoons	cornstarch
3	eggs
1	egg yolk
¹/₄ cup	whipping cream
1¹/₄ teaspoons	vanilla extract
2 teaspoons	peppermint extract
¹/₂ cup	peppermint schnapps
2 drops	red food coloring
1 cup	mint-flavored semisweet chocolate chips

In a large bowl combine cream cheese, sugar, and cornstarch. Beat with an electric mixer till smooth. Add eggs and egg yolk, one at a time, beating well after each addition. Stir in whipping cream and vanilla extract.

Remove half of the mixture and put into a small bowl; stir in peppermint schnapps, peppermint extract, and food coloring. Set aside. Stir mint chocolate chips into the remaining cream cheese mixture.

Pour half of the peppermint mixture over the crust. Spoon half of the chocolate chip mixture over the peppermint mixture. Pour the remaining peppermint mixture over the chocolate chip mixture. Top with remaining chocolate chip mixture. Without disturbing the crust, swirl the blade of a knife through the cake to create a marbling effect.

Bake at 350° for 15 minutes. Lower the temperature to 225° and bake for 1 hour and 10 minutes or till the center no longer looks wet or shiny. Remove the cake from the oven and run a knife around the inside edge of the pan. Turn the oven off; return the cake to the oven for an additional 1 hour. Chill, uncovered, overnight.

White Chocolate Glaze

12 ounces	white chocolate
2 tablespoons	whipping cream
3 ounces	semisweet chocolate
1 tablespoon	butter or margarine

In a small saucepan melt white chocolate over low heat, stirring constantly. Stir in whipping cream. Spread white chocolate mixture over cheesecake. Chill. In a small saucepan melt semisweet chocolate and butter or margarine over low heat, stirring constantly. Drizzle over white chocolate mixture. Chill till serving time. Makes 12 to 18 slices.

Mint Almond Swirl Cheesecake

Crème de menthe liqueur and amaretto team up to enliven this luscious dessert cake.

Chocolate Mint Cookie Crust

11	chocolate mint or chocolate sandwich cream cookies, crushed
3 tablespoons	chopped almonds, toasted
3 tablespoons	butter or margarine, melted

In a small bowl stir together crushed cookies and almonds. Stir in melted butter or margarine till well combined. Press crumb mixture evenly onto the bottom of a greased 9-inch springform pan.

Mint Almond Filling

24 ounces	cream cheese
3/4 cup	sugar
2 tablespoons	whipping cream
5 teaspoons	cornstarch
4	eggs
1	egg yolk
1 1/4 teaspoons	vanilla extract
1/4 cup	green crème de menthe liqueur
1/4 cup	amaretto

In a large bowl combine cream cheese, sugar, whippping cream, and cornstarch. Beat with an electric mixer till smooth. Add eggs and egg yolk, one at a time, beating well after each addition. Beat in vanilla extract.

Remove half of the mixture and put into a small bowl; stir in crème de menthe. Set aside. Stir amaretto into the remaining cream cheese mixture.

Pour half of the amaretto mixture over the crust. Spoon half of the crème de menthe mixture over the amaretto mixture. Pour the remaining amaretto mixture over the crème de menthe mixture. Top with remaining crème de menthe mixture. Without disturbing the crust, swirl the blade of a knife through the cake to create a marbling effect.

Bake at 350° for 15 minutes. Lower the temperature to 200° and bake for 1 hour and 10 minutes or till the center no longer looks wet or shiny. Remove the cake from the oven and run a knife around the inside edge of the pan. Chill, uncovered, overnight. Makes 12 to 18 slices.

Chocolate Mint Cheesecake

This cheesecake is as cool and refreshing as mint chocolate chip ice cream.

Chocolate Cookie Crust

11	chocolate sandwich cream cookies, crushed
3 tablespoons	butter or margarine

In a small bowl stir together crushed cookies and melted butter or margarine till well combined. Press crumb mixture evenly onto the bottom of a 9-inch springform pan.

Minty Chocolate Filling

24 ounces	cream cheese
³/₄ cup	sugar
5 teaspoons	cornstarch
3	eggs
1	egg yolk
¹/₃ cup	green crème de menthe liqueur
¹/₃ cup	white crème de cacao
1 ¹/₄ teaspoons	vanilla extract
3	chocolate mint sandwich cream cookies, coarsely crushed

In a large bowl combine cream cheese, sugar, and cornstarch. Beat with an electric mixer till smooth. Add eggs and egg yolk, one at a time, beating well after each addition. Beat in crème de menthe, crème de cacao, and vanilla extract. Stir in crushed cookies. Pour the cream cheese mixture over the crust.

Bake at 350° for 10 minutes. Lower the temperature to 200° and bake for 1 hour and 10 minutes or till the center no longer looks wet or shiny. Remove the cake from the oven and run a knife around the inside edge of the pan. Chill, uncovered, overnight.

Nut Cheesecakes

Almond Coffee Cheesecake

This is the perfect choice to serve at a sophisticated dinner party.

Chocolate Wafer Crust

1³/₄ cup	crushed chocolate wafers
3 tablespoons	chopped almonds, toasted
3 tablespoons	butter or margarine, melted
1 teaspoon	instant coffee

In a small bowl stir together crushed wafers and chopped almonds. Stir together melted butter or margarine and instant coffee; stir into wafer mixture till well combined. Press crumb mixture evenly onto the bottom of a greased 9-inch springform pan.

Almond Coffee Filling

24 ounces	cream cheese
³/₄ cup	sugar
¹/₄ cup	whipping cream
5 teaspoons	cornstarch
4	eggs
1	egg yolk
¹/₄ cup plus 1 tablespoon	amaretto
¹/₂ teaspoon	almond extract
1 teaspoon	hot water
³/₄ teaspoon	instant coffee
¹/₄ cup	coffee-flavored liqueur

In a large bowl combine cream cheese, sugar, and cornstarch. Beat with an electric mixer till smooth. Add eggs and egg yolk, one at a time, beating well after each addition.

Remove half of the mixture and put into a small bowl; stir in amaretto and almond extract. Set aside. Stir together hot water and instant coffee. Stir coffee and liqueur into the remaining cream cheese mixture.

Pour half of the amaretto mixture over the crust. Spoon half of the coffee mixture over the amaretto mixture. Pour the remaining amaretto mixture over the coffee mixture. Top with remaining coffee mixture. Without disturbing the crust, swirl the blade of a knife through the cake to create a marbling effect.

Bake at 350° for 15 minutes. Lower the temperature to 200° and bake for 1 hour and 10 minutes or till the center no longer looks wet or shiny. Remove the cake from the oven and run a knife around the inside edge of the pan. Turn the oven off; return the cake to the oven for an additional 1 hour. Chill, uncovered, overnight.

Easy Almond Topping

1 cup	whipping cream
1 tablespoon	sugar
	Chocolate coffee beans
	Chopped almonds

In a small bowl beat whipping cream and sugar with an electric mixer till stiff peaks form. Spread whipped cream mixture over cheesecake. Garnish with coffee beans and chopped almonds. Chill till serving time. Makes 12 to 18 slices.

California Amaretto Cheesecake

Californians love to combine the flavors of almonds, orange, and chocolate. You'll enjoy them together in this pretty cheesecake.

Chocolate Cookie Crust

11	milk chocolate sandwich cream cookies, crushed
3 tablespoons	butter or margarine, melted

In a small bowl stir together crushed cookies and melted butter or margarine till well combined. Press crumb mixture evenly onto the bottom of a greased 9-inch springform pan.

Amaretto Filling

24 ounces	cream cheese
2/3 cup	sugar
5 teaspoons	flour
3	eggs
1	egg yolk
1/4 cup	sour cream
1/2 cup	amaretto
1 teaspoon	almond extract
1/4 cup	chopped almonds, toasted

In a large bowl combine cream cheese, sugar, and flour. Beat with an electric mixer till smooth. Add eggs and egg yolk, one at a time, beating well after each addition. Beat in sour cream, amaretto, and almond extract. Stir in chopped almonds. Pour the cream cheese mixture over the crust.

Bake at 350° for 15 minutes. Lower the temperature to 200° and bake for 1 hour and 10 minutes or till the center no longer looks wet or shiny. Remove the cake from the oven and run a knife around the inside edge of the pan. Turn the oven off; return the cake to the oven for an additional 30 minutes. Chill, uncovered, overnight.

Chocolate Orange Topping

1/3 cup	orange marmalade
1/4 cup	frozen orange juice concentrate, thawed
2 teaspoons	lemon juice
1 tablespoon	cornstarch
	Fresh fruit, sliced
	Chocolate curls

In a small saucepan stir together marmalade, orange juice concentrate, lemon juice, and cornstarch. Cook and stir till thickened and bubbly. Cook and stir 2 minutes more. Pour over cheesecake. Garnish with fruit and chocolate curls. Chill till serving time. Makes 12 to 18 slices.

Baklava Cheesecake

Phyllo dough is used for the crust in this Middle Eastern inspired cheesecake. Look for it in your grocer's freezer case.

Phyllo Crust

3 sheets	frozen phyllo dough, thawed
3 tablespoons	butter or margarine, melted

Place 1 sheet of phyllo on the bottom of the cheesecake pan, folding to fit. Brush with some of the melted butter or margarine. Repeat layering and brushing with remaining phyllo dough and butter or margarine. Cover with plastic wrap or a damp towel. Set aside.

Baklava Filling

24 ounces	cream cheese
2/3 cup	sugar
1/4 cup	honey
5 teaspoons	cornstarch
4	eggs
1/4 cup	rose water or rose syrup*
1 teaspoon	finely shredded lemon peel
1/3 cup	coarsely chopped walnuts
1/4 cup	flaked or freshly grated coconut
2 tablespoons	chopped almonds, toasted

In a large bowl combine cream cheese, sugar, honey, and cornstarch. Beat with an electric mixer till smooth. Add eggs one at a time, beating well after each addition. Beat in rose water or syrup and lemon peel. Stir in walnuts, coconut, and almonds. Pour the cream cheese mixture over the crust.

Bake at 350° for 15 minutes. Lower the temperature to 225° and bake for 1 hour and 10 minutes or till the center no longer looks wet or shiny. Remove the cake from the oven and run a knife around the inside edge of the pan. Turn the oven off; return the cake to the oven for an additional 1 hour. Chill, uncovered, overnight.

---

*Look for rose water or rose syrup at a Middle Eastern food store.

Nutty Coconut Topping

1/3 cup	sugar
1/4 cup	water
1 tablespoon	honey
2 teaspoons	cornstarch
1 teaspoon	rose water or rose syrup
1/2 cup	flaked or freshly grated coconut
1/4 cup	coarsely chopped walnuts
2 tablespoons	coarsely chopped almonds, toasted

In a small saucepan stir together sugar, water, honey, cornstarch, and rose water or syrup. Cook and stir till thickened and bubbly. Cook, uncovered, for 20 minutes more, stirring occasionally. Stir in the coconut, walnuts, and almonds. Spread the warm coconut mixture over the cake. Chill till serving time. Makes 12 to 18 slices.

Maple Pecan Cheesecake

For a special treat, use real maple syrup instead of maple-flavored syrup.

Vanilla Cookie Crust

11	vanilla sandwich cream cookies, crushed
3 tablespoons	butter or margarine, melted

In a small bowl stir together crushed cookies and melted butter or margarine till well combined. Press crumb mixture evenly onto the bottom of a greased 9-inch springform pan.

Maple Pecan Filling

24 ounces	cream cheese
3/4 cup	light brown sugar
1/3 cup	maple or maple-flavored syrup
5 teaspoons	cornstarch
3	eggs
1	egg yolk
2 teaspoons	vanilla extract
2/3 cup	chopped pecans

In a large bowl combine cream cheese, sugar, syrup, and cornstarch. Beat with an electric mixer till smooth. Add eggs and egg yolk, one at a time, beating well after each addition. Beat in vanilla extract. Stir in pecans. Pour the cream cheese mixture over the crust.

Bake at 350° for 15 minutes. Lower the temperature to 225° and bake for 1 hour and 15 minutes or till the center no longer looks wet or shiny. Remove the cake from the oven and run a knife around the inside edge of the pan. Turn the oven off; return the cake to the oven for an additional 1 hour. Chill, uncovered, overnight. Makes 12 to 18 slices.

Peanut Butter Cheesecakes

Peanut Butter and Chocolate Cheesecake

Attention all peanut butter and chocolate addicts: you'll go wild over this decadent cheesecake.

Chocolate Peanut Butter Crust

1 cup	finely crushed chocolate wafers
1 cup	finely crushed crisp peanut butter cookies
1/4 cup	finely chopped peanuts
1/2 cup	butter or margarine, melted

In a medium bowl stir together crushed chocolate wafers, crushed peanut butter cookies, and chopped peanuts. Add melted butter or margarine and stir till well combined. Press crumb mixture evenly onto the bottom and up the sides of a 9-inch springform pan. Set aside.

Chocolate Peanut Butter Filling

24 ounces	cream cheese
2/3 cup	dark brown sugar
1 tablespoon	cornstarch
1 cup	semisweet chocolate chips, melted
3/4 cup	peanut butter
5	eggs
1 teaspoon	vanilla extract
2/3 cup	chopped peanuts

In a large bowl combine cream cheese, brown sugar, and cornstarch. Beat with an electric mixer till smooth. Beat in melted chocolate chips and peanut butter. Add eggs, one at a time, beating well after each addition. Beat in vanilla extract. Stir in chopped peanuts. Pour cream cheese mixture over crust.

Bake at 350° for 15 minutes. Lower the temperature to 225° and bake for 1 hour and 10 minutes or until the center no longer looks wet or shiny. Remove the cake from the oven and run a knife around the inside edge of the pan. Turn the oven off; return the cake to the oven for an additional 30 minutes. Chill, uncovered, overnight.

Peanut Butter and Chocolate Swirl Topping

8 ounces	white chocolate, coarsely chopped
2 tablespoons	peanut butter
1 ounce	semisweet chocolate, melted

In a small saucepan melt white chocolate and peanut butter over low heat, stirring constantly. Cool to lukewarm. Pour peanut butter mixture over cheesecake. Drizzle parallel strips of melted semisweet chocolate over peanut butter mixture. Using a knife, draw the dull side of the tip across the chocolate. Chill till serving time. Makes 12 to 18 slices.

Peanut Butter and Banana Cheesecake

This is for those of you who relish peanut butter and banana sandwiches. Here's a delicious dessert to satisfy your cravings.

Peanut Butter Cookie Crust

11	peanut butter sandwich cream cookies, crushed
3 tablespoons	chopped peanuts
3 tablespoons	butter or margarine, melted

In a small bowl stir together crushed cookies and peanuts. Stir in melted butter or margarine till well combined. Press crumb mixture evenly onto the bottom of a greased 9-inch springform pan.

Peanut Butter and Banana Filling

24 ounces	cream cheese
2/3 cup	dark brown sugar
2/3 cup	sour cream
3 teaspoons	cornstarch
3	eggs
1	egg yolk
2/3 cup	mashed banana
1 teaspoon	vanilla extract
1 cup	creamy peanut butter
1/3 cup	chopped peanuts

In a large bowl combine cream cheese, brown sugar, sour cream, and cornstarch. Beat with an electric mixer till smooth. Add eggs and egg yolk, one at a time, beating well after each addition. Beat in vanilla extract. Remove 2/3 cup of the mixture and put into a small bowl; stir in mashed banana. Set aside. Stir peanut butter and peanuts into the remaining cream cheese mixture.

Pour half of the peanut butter mixture over the crust. Spoon on the banana mixture. Pour the remaining peanut butter mixture over the banana mixture.

Bake at 350° for 15 minutes. Lower the temperature to 200° and bake for 1 hour and 10 minutes or till the center no longer looks wet or shiny. Remove the cake from the oven and run a knife around the inside edge of the pan. Turn the oven off; return the cake to the oven for an additional 1 hour. Chill, uncovered, overnight.

Chocolate Banana Topping

1 cup	whipping cream
1 tablespoon	sugar
	Chocolate-dipped banana slices

In a small bowl beat whipping cream and sugar with an electric mixer till stiff peaks form. Pipe whipped cream mixture around the edge of the cheesecake. Garnish with chocolate-dipped banana slices. Chill till serving time. Makes 12 to 18 slices.

Peanut Butter and Jelly Cheesecake

It's better than the sandwich!

Peanut Butter Cookie Crust

11	peanut butter sandwich cream cookies, crushed
3 tablespoons	chopped peanuts
3 tablespoons	butter or margarine, melted

In a small bowl stir together crushed cookies and peanuts. Stir in melted butter or margarine till well combined. Press crumb mixture evenly onto the bottom of a greased 9-inch springform pan.

Peanut Butter Filling

24 ounces	cream cheese
2/3 cup	dark brown sugar
3 teaspoons	cornstarch
4	eggs
1	egg yolk
1 cup	sour cream
2/3 cup	whipping cream
2 teaspoons	vanilla extract
1 cup	creamy peanut butter
2/3 cup	chopped peanuts

In a large bowl combine cream cheese, brown sugar, and cornstarch. Beat with an electric mixer till smooth. Add eggs and egg yolk, one at a time, beating well after each addition. Stir in sour cream, whipping cream, and vanilla extract. Stir in peanut butter and peanuts. Pour the cream cheese mixture over the crust.

   Bake at 350° for 15 minutes. Lower the temperature to 200° and bake for 1 hour and 10 minutes or till the center no longer looks wet or shiny. Remove the cake from the oven and run a knife around the inside edge of the pan. Turn the oven off; return the cake to the oven for an additional 1 hour. Chill, uncovered, overnight.

Easy Jelly Topping

1 cup	grape or strawberry jelly

In a small saucepan heat jelly till warm. Spread warm topping over cheesecake. Chill till serving time. Makes 12 to 18 slices.

Vanilla Cheesecakes

Super New York-Style Cheesecake

This classic dessert can also be made with a graham cracker crust by substituting graham cracker crumbs for the crushed vanilla wafers.

Vanilla Wafer Crust

1³/₄ cups	finely crushed vanilla wafers
¹/₂ cup	butter or margarine, melted

In a small bowl stir together crushed wafers and melted butter or margarine. Stir till well combined. Press crumb mixture evenly onto the bottom and up the sides of a greased 9-inch springform pan. Set aside.

New York Filling

32 ounces	cream cheese
1 cup	sugar
3 tablespoons	flour
5	eggs
¹/₃ cup	whipping cream
1 teaspoon	finely shredded orange peel
1 teaspoon	finely shredded lemon peel
1 teaspoon	vanilla extract
1 cup	sour cream
2 tablespoons	sugar
¹/₂ teaspoon	vanilla extract

In a large bowl combine cream cheese, 1 cup sugar, and flour. Beat with an electric mixer till smooth. Add eggs, one at a time, beating well after each addition. Stir in whipping cream, orange peel, lemon peel, and 1 teaspoon vanilla extract. Pour the cream cheese mixture over the crust.

Bake at 350° for 15 minutes. Lower the temperature to 200° and bake for 1 hour and 20 minutes or till the center no longer looks wet or shiny. Remove the cake from the oven. Stir together sour cream, 2 tablespoons sugar, and ¹/₂ teaspoon vanilla extract. Spread over warm cheesecake.

Return cheesecake to the oven and bake for 15 minutes more. Remove from oven and run a knife around the inside edge of the pan. Do not chill cheesecake.

Sour Cream Topping

1 cup	sour cream
1 tablespoon	sugar
1 teaspoon	vanilla extract

In a small bowl stir together sour cream, sugar, and vanilla extract. Spread sour cream mixture over warm cheesecake. Bake at 350° for an additional 15 minutes. Chill, uncovered, overnight. Makes 12 to 18 slices.

Dutch Vanilla Cheesecake

This cheesecake is richly flavored with vanilla liqueur.

Vanilla Crust

1 1/4 cups	finely crushed vanilla wafers
1/4 cup	butter or margarine, melted

In a small bowl stir together crumbs and melted butter or margarine. Stir till well combined. Press crumb mixture evenly onto the bottom of a 9-inch springform pan. Set aside.

Dutch Vanilla Filling

24 ounces	cream cheese
2/3 cup	sugar
1/2 cup	whipping cream
5 teaspoons	cornstarch
4	eggs
1	egg yolk
1/4 cup	vanilla-flavored liqueur
2 teaspoons	vanilla extract

In a large bowl combine cream cheese, sugar, whippping cream, and cornstarch. Beat with an electric mixer till smooth. Add eggs and egg yolk, one at a time, beating well after each addition. Beat in liqueur and vanilla extract. Pour cream cheese mixture over crust.

Bake at 350° for 15 minutes. Lower the temperature to 200° and bake for 1 hour and 10 minutes or until the center no longer looks wet or shiny. Remove the cake from the oven and run a knife around the inside edge of the pan. Chill, uncovered, overnight.

Cherry Topping

2 17-ounce jars	maraschino cherries
1 tablespoon	cornstarch

Drain cherries, reserving 1 1/2 cups liquid (add water, if necessary, to make a total of 1 1/2 cups liquid). In a small saucepan stir together reserved cherry liquid and cornstarch. Cook and stir till thickened and bubbly. Cook and stir 2 minutes more. Spread 1 cup of the cherry mixture over cheesecake. Set aside remaining cherry mixture. Arrange cherries on top. Chill till serving time.

Easy Whipped Topping

1 cup	whipping cream
1 tablespoon	sugar
1/8 teaspoon	almond extract

Just before serving, in a small bowl beat whipping cream, sugar, and almond extract with an electric mixer till slightly thickened. Reheat remaining cherry mixture in a small saucepan. Pool whipped topping on individual serving plates. Spoon some of the cherry mixture over the whipped topping. Using a knife, gently swirl the mixture to marble it. Place sliced cheesecake on plates. Makes 12 to 18 slices.

Individual Cheesecakes

To remove these miniature cheesecakes from their tart pans, simply freeze them till firm after they are baked. Then pop them out of the pans and chill till serving time.

Vanilla Wafer Crust

1 1/4 cups	finely crushed vanilla wafers
1/4 cup	butter or margarine

In a small bowl stir together crushed wafers and butter and margarine. Press crumb mixture evenly onto the bottom of 12 small tart pans. Set aside.

Filling

32 ounces	cream cheese
1 cup	sugar
3 tablespoons	cornstarch
5	eggs
1/3 cup	whipping cream
1 teaspoon	finely shredded lemon peel
1 teaspoon	finely shredded orange peel
1 teaspoon	vanilla extract

In a large bowl combine cream cheese, sugar, and cornstarch. Beat with an electric mixer till smooth. Add eggs, one at a time, beating well after each addition. Stir in whipping cream, lemon peel, orange peel, and vanilla extract. Spoon cream cheese mixture into each tart pan.

Bake at 225° for 35 to 45 minutes or till the center springs back when touched. Remove the tart pans from the oven and cool. Place tart pans in freezer about 1 hour or till firm. Remove individual cheesecakes from tart pans. Chill, uncovered, overnight.

Lemon Sauce

¹/₄ cup	sugar
1 tablespoon	cornstarch
1 teaspoon	finely shredded lemon peel
¹/₂ cup	water
1 tablespoon	lemon juice
	Yellow food coloring (optional)

In a small saucepan combine sugar, cornstarch, and lemon peel. Stir in water and lemon juice. Cook and stir till thickened and bubbly. Cook and stir 2 minutes more. Stir in food coloring, if desired. Keep warm while preparing Raspberry Sauce.

Raspberry Sauce

¹/₂ cup	raspberries
¹/₃ cup	water
¹/₄ cup	sugar
1 tablespoon	cornstarch

In a blender container or food processor combine raspberries and water. Cover and blend till smooth. Sieve berry mixture. In a small saucepan combine sugar and cornstarch. Stir in berry mixture. Cook and stir till thickened and bubbly. Cook and stir 2 minutes more. Drizzle warm sauce over cheesecakes. Drizzle warm Lemon Sauce over cheesecakes. Makes 12 individual cheesecakes.

Honey Vanilla Cheesecake

This cheesecake is similar to the Dutch Vanilla Cheesecake except it is endowed with a good dose of honey.

Vanilla Cookie Crust

11	vanilla sandwich cream cookies, crushed
3 tablespoons	chopped almonds, toasted
3 tablespoons	butter or margarine, melted

In a small bowl stir together crushed cookies and chopped almonds. Stir in melted butter or margarine till well combined. Press crumb mixture evenly onto the bottom of a greased 9-inch springform pan.

Honey Vanilla Filling

24 ounces	cream cheese
²/₃ cup	sugar
3 tablespoons	honey
2 tablespoons	whipping cream
5 teaspoons	cornstarch
4	eggs
1	egg yolk
¹/₂ cup	vanilla-flavored liqueur
2 tablespoons	amaretto
2 teaspoons	vanilla extract
³/₄ teaspoon	almond extract
¹/₃ cup	chopped almonds, toasted

In a large bowl combine cream cheese, sugar, honey, whipping cream, and cornstarch. Beat with an electric mixer till smooth. Add eggs and egg yolk, one at a time, beating well after each addition. Beat in liqueur, amaretto, vanilla extract, and almond extract. Stir in almonds. Pour the cream cheese mixture over the crust.

Bake at 350° for 15 minutes. Lower the temperature to 200° and bake for 1 hour and 10 minutes or till the center no longer looks wet or shiny. Remove the cake from the oven and run a knife around the inside edge of the pan. Turn the oven off; return the cake to the oven for an additional 1 hour. Chill, uncovered, overnight.

Easy Vanilla Topping

1 cup	whipping cream
1 tablespoon	sugar
1 tablespoon	vanilla-flavored liqueur
	Whole almonds

In a small bowl beat whipping cream, sugar, and vanilla-flavored liqueur with an electric mixer till stiff peaks form. Pipe whipped cream mixture around the edge of the cheesecake. Garnish with almonds. Chill till serving time. Makes 12 to 18 slices.

Guilt-Free Cheesecakes

The light cheesecakes in this chapter cut calories and cholesterol without sacrificing the rich taste a cheesecake is known for. These recipes cut calories by 56.8% and cut cholesterol by 85.8%. While a piece of regular cheesecake, at 18 pieces per cake, has about 289 calories and 138 mg cholesterol, a piece of guilt-free cheesecake contains about 125 calories and 20 mg cholesterol. The key to this healthier cheesecake is in the replacements: tofu, egg whites, and sugar substitutes.

A soybean curd, tofu is a filler that replaces a portion of the cream cheese and the other dairy products. Because it does not have a flavor of its own, tofu picks up whatever flavor is used in the cake. Therefore, these cakes require more flavoring than a regular cheesecake to compensate for the blandness of the tofu. Tofu has about 20 calories per ounce and no cholesterol.

Egg whites also make for lighter cheesecakes. As opposed to egg yolks, egg whites have no cholesterol. And they have only one-fourth the calories of whole eggs. (Egg yolks are the problematic part of eggs, having 272 mg cholesterol and 63 calories.) Sugar substitutes have 88% fewer calories than sugar, although neither sugar nor sugar substitutes contains cholesterol.

These ingredients are delicate, and the cakes require a little extra care as you prepare them. One potential problem is cracks, but, while regular cheesecake cracks may be large, these cracks are hairline size and easily smoothed with the warm edge of a knife. To prevent these cracks, do not overbeat the egg whites.

Care also must be taken to avoid hot ovens with these cheesecakes. Because of the lower baking temperature, the cake may seem too liquid at the end of its cooking time, but it will set in the turned-off oven. If it does not set, you can easily firm up the cheesecake in the refrigerator overnight.

Fresh Strawberry Cheesecake

Fresh strawberries are a must! They are available almost year round but are at their best from April through July.

Vanilla Cookie Crust

| 11 | vanilla sandwich cream cookies, crushed |
| 3 tablespoons | butter or margarine, melted |

In a small bowl stir together crushed cookies and melted butter or margarine till well combined. Press crumb mixture evenly onto the bottom of a greased 9-inch springform pan.

Strawberry Filling

16 ounces	light cream cheese
12 ounces	tofu, well drained
1/2 cup	granulated sugar replacement
1/4 cup	strawberry schnapps
2 tablespoons	cornstarch
2 teaspoons	vanilla extract
6	egg whites
1 cup	sliced strawberries

In a large bowl combine cream cheese, tofu, sugar replacement, strawberry schnapps, cornstarch, and vanilla extract. Beat with an electric mixer till smooth. Stir in egg whites and strawberries. Pour the cream cheese mixture over the crust.

Bake at 225° for 1 hour and 20 minutes or till the center no longer looks wet or shiny. Remove the cake from the oven and run a knife around the inside edge of the pan. Turn the oven off; return the cake to the oven for an additional 2 hours. Chill, uncovered, overnight. Makes 18 slices.

Low-Calorie Amaretto Cheesecake

Toast the almonds on a baking sheet in a 350° oven about 10 minutes or till light brown.

Chocolate Cookie Crust

11	chocolate sandwich cream cookies, crushed
2 tablespoons	chopped almonds, toasted
3 tablespoons	butter or margarine, melted

In a small bowl stir together crushed cookies and almonds. Stir in melted butter or margarine till well combined. Press crumb mixture evenly onto the bottom of a greased 9-inch springform pan.

Amaretto Filling

16 ounces	light cream cheese
12 ounces	tofu, well drained
1/2 cup	granulated sugar replacement
1/4 cup	amaretto
2 tablespoons	cornstarch
2 teaspoons	vanilla extract
2 teaspoons	almond extract
12	egg whites

In a large bowl combine cream cheese, tofu, sugar replacement, amaretto, cornstarch, vanilla extract, and almond extract. Beat with an electric mixer till smooth. Stir in egg whites. Pour the cream cheese mixture over the crust.

Bake at 225° for 1 hour and 20 minutes or till the center no longer looks wet or shiny. Remove the cake from the oven and run a knife around the inside edge of the pan. Turn the oven off; return the cake to the oven for an additional 2 hours. Chill, uncovered, overnight. Makes 18 slices.

Light Lime Cheesecake

Make this refreshing cheesecake for St. Patrick's Day and stir 2 or 3 drops of green food coloring into the batter.

Lemon Cookie Crust

| 11 | lemon sandwich cream cookies, crushed |
| 3 tablespoons | butter or margarine, melted |

In a small bowl stir together crushed cookies and melted butter or margarine till well combined. Press crumb mixture evenly onto the bottom of a greased 9-inch springform pan.

Lime Filling

16 ounces	light cream cheese
12 ounces	tofu, well drained
½ cup	granulated sugar replacement
¼ cup	frozen limeade concentrate, thawed
2 tablespoons	cornstarch
2 teaspoons	vanilla extract
1 teaspoon	finely shredded lime peel
11	egg whites

In a large bowl combine cream cheese, tofu, sugar replacement, limeade concentrate, cornstarch, vanilla extract, and lime peel. Beat with an electric mixer till smooth. Stir in egg whites. Pour the cream cheese mixture over the crust.

Bake at 225° for 1 hour and 20 minutes or till the center no longer looks wet or shiny. Remove the cake from the oven and run a knife around the inside edge of the pan. Turn the oven off; return the cake to the oven for an additional 2 hours. Chill, uncovered, overnight. Makes 18 slices.

Coffee Cream Cheesecake

This 12-egg-white cake is light and luscious. Keep in mind that egg whites will separate more easily when they are cold.

Vanilla Cookie Crust

| 11 | vanilla sandwich cream cookies, crushed |
| 3 tablespoons | butter or margarine, melted |

In a small bowl stir together crushed cookies and melted butter or margarine till well combined. Press crumb mixture evenly onto the bottom of a greased 9-inch springform pan.

Coffee Cream Filling

1 tablespoon	instant coffee
1 tablespoon	hot water
16 ounces	light cream cheese
12 ounces	tofu, well drained
½ cup	granulated sugar replacement
¼ cup	coffee-flavored liqueur
2 tablespoons	cornstarch
2 teaspoons	vanilla extract
12	egg whites

Stir together instant coffee and hot water till coffee dissolves. In a large bowl combine coffee, cream cheese, tofu, sugar replacement, coffee-flavored liqueur, cornstarch, and vanilla extract. Beat with an electric mixer till smooth. Stir in egg whites. Pour the cream cheese mixture over the crust.

Bake at 225° for 1 hour and 20 minutes or till the center no longer looks wet or shiny. Remove the cake from the oven and run a knife around the inside edge of the pan. Turn the oven off; return the cake to the oven for an additional 2 hours. Chill, uncovered, overnight. Makes 18 slices.

Slim Chocolate Mint Cheesecake

Bet your guests will never know that this is a reduced-calorie cheesecake!

Chocolate Mint Cookie Crust

11	chocolate mint or chocolate sandwich cream cookies, crushed
3 tablespoons	butter or margarine, melted

In a small bowl stir together crushed cookies and melted butter or margarine till well combined. Press crumb mixture evenly onto the bottom of a greased 9-inch springform pan.

Chocolate Mint Filling

16 ounces	light cream cheese
12 ounces	tofu, well drained
3/4 cup	granulated sugar replacement
1/3 cup	unsweetened cocoa powder
1/4 cup	crème de cacao
2 tablespoons	cornstarch
2 teaspoons	vanilla extract
1 teaspoon	mint extract
12	egg whites

In a large bowl combine cream cheese, tofu, sugar replacement, cocoa powder, crème de cacao, cornstarch, vanilla extract, and mint extract. Beat with an electric mixer till smooth. Stir in egg whites. Pour the cream cheese mixture over the crust.

Bake at 225° for 1 hour and 20 minutes or till the center no longer looks wet or shiny. Remove the cake from the oven and run a knife around the inside edge of the pan. Turn the oven off; return the cake to the oven for an additional 2 hours. Chill, uncovered, overnight. Makes 18 slices.

Caramel Praline Cheesecake

Vanilla Cookie Crust

11	vanilla sandwich cream cookies, crushed
3 tablespoons	butter or margarine, melted

In a small bowl stir together crushed cookies and melted butter or margarine till well combined. Press crumb mixture evenly onto the bottom of a greased 9-inch springform pan.

Caramel Praline Filling

16 ounces	light cream cheese
12 ounces	tofu, well drained
1/2 cup	brown sugar replacement
1/4 cup	praline-flavored liqueur
2 tablespoons	cornstarch
2 teaspoons	vanilla extract
12	egg whites

In a large bowl combine cream cheese, tofu, sugar replacement, liqueur, cornstarch, and vanilla extract. Beat with an electric mixer till smooth. Stir in egg whites. Pour the cream cheese mixture over the crust.

Bake at 225° for 1 hour and 20 minutes or till the center no longer looks wet or shiny. Remove the cake from the oven and run a knife around the inside edge of the pan. Turn the oven off; return the cake to the oven for an additional 2 hours. Chill, uncovered, overnight. Makes 18 slices.

Skinny Banana Split Cheesecake

Banana, pineapple, and strawberries are stirred into the light cheesecake filling.

Vanilla Cookie Crust

11	vanilla sandwich cream cookies, crushed
3 tablespoons	butter or margarine, melted

In a small bowl stir together crushed cookies and melted butter or margarine till well combined. Press crumb mixture evenly onto the bottom of a greased 9-inch springform pan.

Banana Split Filling

16 ounces	light cream cheese
12 ounces	tofu, well drained
1/2 cup	granulated sugar replacement
1/3 cup	puréed banana (1 small banana)
1/4 cup	banana schnapps
2 tablespoons	cornstarch
2 teaspoons	vanilla extract
7	egg whites
1/2 cup	juice-pack crushed pineapple, drained
1/2 cup	sliced strawberries

In a large bowl combine cream cheese, tofu, sugar replacement, puréed banana, banana schnapps, cornstarch, and vanilla extract. Beat with an electric mixer till smooth. Stir in egg whites, pineapple, and strawberries. Pour the cream cheese mixture over the crust.

Bake at 225° for 1 hour and 20 minutes or till the center no longer looks wet or shiny. Remove the cake from the oven and run a knife around the inside edge of the pan. Turn the oven off; return the cake to the oven for an additional 2 hours. Chill, uncovered, overnight. Makes 18 slices.

Fresh Tangerine Cheesecake

You'll find fresh tangerines at your grocery store from November to May.

Orange-Pineapple Cookie Crust

11	orange-pineapple or vanilla sandwich cream cookies, crushed
3 tablespoons	butter or margarine, melted

In a small bowl stir together crushed cookies and melted butter or margarine till well combined. Press crumb mixture evenly onto the bottom of a greased 9-inch springform pan.

Tangerine Filling

16 ounces	light cream cheese
12 ounces	tofu, well drained
1/2 cup	granulated sugar replacement
1/4 cup	frozen tangerine or orange juice concentrate, thawed
2 tablespoons	cornstarch
2 teaspoons	vanilla extract
1 teaspoon	finely shredded orange peel
12	egg whites
2 medium	tangerines, peeled and chopped

In a large bowl combine cream cheese, tofu, sugar replacement, tangerine or orange juice concentrate, cornstarch, vanilla extract, and orange peel. Beat with an electric mixer till smooth. Stir in egg whites and tangerines. Pour the cream cheese mixture over the crust.

Bake at 225° for 1 hour and 20 minutes or till the center no longer looks wet or shiny. Remove the cake from the oven and run a knife around the inside edge of the pan. Turn the oven off; return the cake to the oven for an additional 2 hours. Chill, uncovered, overnight. Makes 18 slices.

Tropical Blend Cheesecake

Garnish this light cheesecake with sliced starfruit, papaya, guava, or mango.

Lemon Cookie Crust

11	lemon sandwich cream cookies, crushed
3 tablespoons	butter or margarine, melted

In a small bowl stir together crushed cookies and melted butter or margarine till well combined. Press crumb mixture evenly onto the bottom of a greased 9-inch springform pan.

Tropical Blend Filling

16 ounces	light cream cheese
12 ounces	tofu, well drained
1/2 cup	granulated sugar replacement
1/4 cup	frozen tropical fruit juice concentrate, thawed
2 tablespoons	cornstarch
1 teaspoon	finely shredded lime or lemon peel
1 teaspoon	finely shredded orange peel
1/2 teaspoon	coconut extract
1/2 teaspoon	pineapple extract
1/8 teaspoon	almond extract
11	egg whites
	Fresh tropical fruit, sliced

In a large bowl combine cream cheese, tofu, sugar replacement, fruit juice concentrate, cornstarch, lime or lemon peel, orange peel, coconut extract, pineapple extract, and almond extract. Beat with an electric mixer till smooth. Stir in egg whites. Pour the cream cheese mixture over the crust.

Bake at 225° for 1 hour and 20 minutes or till the center no longer looks wet or shiny. Remove the cake from the oven and run a knife around the inside edge of the pan. Turn the oven off; return the cake to the oven for an additional 2 hours. Chill, uncovered, overnight. Garnish with fresh fruit. Chill till serving time. Makes 18 slices.

Light Limon Cheesecake

Lemon Cookie Crust

11	lemon or vanilla sandwich cream cookies, crushed
3 tablespoons	butter or margarine, melted

In a small bowl stir together crushed cookies and melted butter or margarine till well combined. Press crumb mixture evenly onto the bottom of a greased 9-inch springform pan.

Limon Filling

16 ounces	light cream cheese
12 ounces	tofu, well drained
1/2 cup	granulated sugar replacement
2 tablespoons	cornstarch
2 tablespoons	frozen limeade concentrate, thawed
2 tablespoons	frozen lemonade concentrate, thawed
2 teaspoons	vanilla extract
1 teaspoon	finely shredded lime peel
1 teaspoon	finely shredded lemon peel
11	egg whites

In a large bowl combine cream cheese, tofu, sugar replacement, cornstarch, limeade concentrate, lemonade concentrate, vanilla extract, lime peel, and lemon peel. Beat with an electric mixer till smooth. Stir in egg whites. Pour the cream cheese mixture over the crust.

Bake at 225° for 1 hour and 20 minutes or till the center no longer looks wet or shiny. Remove the cake from the oven and run a knife around the inside edge of the pan. Turn the oven off; return the cake to the oven for an additional 2 hours. Chill, uncovered, overnight. Makes 18 slices.

Tangy Orange Cheesecake

Pineapple-Orange Cookie Crust

11	pineapple-orange or vanilla sandwich cream cookies, crushed
3 tablespoons	butter or margarine, melted

In a small bowl stir together crushed cookies and melted butter or margarine till well combined. Press crumb mixture evenly onto the bottom of a greased 9-inch springform pan.

Tangy Orange Filling

16 ounces	light cream cheese
12 ounces	tofu, well drained
1/2 cup	granulated sugar replacement
1/4 cup	frozen orange juice concentrate, thawed
2 tablespoons	cornstarch
2 teaspoons	vanilla extract
1 teaspoon	finely shredded orange peel
12	egg whites
	Fresh orange slices

In a large bowl combine cream cheese, tofu, sugar replacement, orange juice concentrate, cornstarch, vanilla extract, and orange peel. Beat with an electric mixer till smooth. Stir in egg whites. Pour the cream cheese mixture over the crust.

Bake at 225° for 1 hour and 20 minutes or till the center no longer looks wet or shiny. Remove the cake from the oven and run a knife around the inside edge of the pan. Turn the oven off; return the cake to the oven for an additional 2 hours. Chill, uncovered, overnight. Garnish with orange slices. Makes 18 slices.

Slice of Lemon Cheesecake

Lemon Cookie Crust

11	lemon or vanilla sandwich cream cookies, crushed
3 tablespoons	butter or margarine, melted

In a small bowl stir together crushed cookies and melted butter or margarine till well combined. Press crumb mixture evenly onto the bottom of a greased 9-inch springform pan.

Lemon Filling

16 ounces	light cream cheese
12 ounces	tofu, well drained
1/2 cup	granulated sugar replacement
1/4 cup	lemonade concentrate
2 tablespoons	cornstarch
2 teaspoons	vanilla extract
1 teaspoon	finely shredded lemon peel
11	egg whites
	Fresh lemon slices

In a large bowl combine cream cheese, tofu, sugar replacement, lemonade concentrate, cornstarch, vanilla extract, and lemon peel. Beat with an electric mixer till smooth. Stir in egg whites. Pour the cream cheese mixture over the crust.

Bake at 225° for 1 hour and 20 minutes or till the center no longer looks wet or shiny. Remove the cake from the oven and run a knife around the inside edge of the pan. Turn the oven off; return the cake to the oven for an additional 2 hours. Chill, uncovered, overnight. Garnish with lemon slices. Makes 18 slices.

Calorie-Trimmed Coffee Cheesecake

Chocolate Cookie Crust

11	milk chocolate sandwich cream cookies, crushed
3 tablespoons	butter or margarine, melted

In a small bowl stir together crushed cookies and melted butter or margarine till well combined. Press crumb mixture evenly onto the bottom of a greased 9-inch springform pan.

Coffee Filling

1 tablespoon	instant coffee
1 tablespoon	hot water
16 ounces	light cream cheese
12 ounces	tofu, well drained
1/2 cup	granulated sugar replacement
1/4 cup	coffee-flavored liqueur
2 tablespoons	cornstarch
2 teaspoons	vanilla extract
12	egg whites

Stir together instant coffee and hot water till coffee dissolves. In a large bowl combine coffee, cream cheese, tofu, sugar replacement, coffee-flavored liqueur, cornstarch, and vanilla extract. Beat with an electric mixer till smooth. Stir in egg whites. Pour the cream cheese mixture over the crust.

Bake at 225° for 1 hour and 20 minutes or till the center no longer looks wet or shiny. Remove the cake from the oven and run a knife around the inside edge of the pan. Turn the oven off; return the cake to the oven for an additional 2 hours. Chill, uncovered, overnight. Makes 18 slices.

Very Vanilla Cheesecake

Serve this simply delicious dessert with fresh sliced fruit.

Vanilla Cookie Crust

| 11 | vanilla sandwich cream cookies, crushed |
| 3 tablespoons | butter or margarine, melted |

In a small bowl stir together crushed cookies and melted butter or margarine till well combined. Press crumb mixture evenly onto the bottom of a greased 9-inch springform pan.

Vanilla Filling

16 ounces	light cream cheese
12 ounces	tofu, well drained
1/2 cup	granulated sugar replacement
1/4 cup	vanilla-flavored liqueur
2 tablespoons	cornstarch
2 teaspoons	vanilla extract
12	egg whites

In a large bowl combine cream cheese, tofu, sugar replacement, vanilla-flavored liqueur, cornstarch, and vanilla extract. Beat with an electric mixer till smooth. Stir in egg whites. Pour the cream cheese mixture over the crust.

Bake at 225° for 1 hour and 20 minutes or till the center no longer looks wet or shiny. Remove the cake from the oven and run a knife around the inside edge of the pan. Turn the oven off; return the cake to the oven for an additional 2 hours. Chill, uncovered, overnight. Makes 18 slices.

Light Daiquiri Cheesecake

You'll find a lemon crust and lime filling in this refreshing cheesecake.

Lemon Cookie Crust

| 11 | lemon sandwich cream cookies, crushed |
| 3 tablespoons | butter or margarine, melted |

In a small bowl stir together crushed cookies and melted butter or margarine till well combined. Press crumb mixture evenly onto the bottom of a greased 9-inch springform pan.

Daiquiri Filling

16 ounces	light cream cheese
12 ounces	tofu, well drained
1/2 cup	granulated sugar replacement
2 tablespoons	cornstarch
2 tablespoons	frozen limeade concentrate, thawed
1 tablespoon	rum
2 teaspoons	vanilla extract
1 teaspoon	finely shredded lemon peel
11	egg whites

In a large bowl combine cream cheese, tofu, sugar replacement, cornstarch, limeade concentrate, rum, vanilla extract, and lemon peel. Beat with an electric mixer till smooth. Stir in egg whites. Pour the cream cheese mixture over the crust.

Bake at 225° for 1 hour and 20 minutes or till the center no longer looks wet or shiny. Remove the cake from the oven and run a knife around the inside edge of the pan. Turn the oven off; return the cake to the oven for an additional 2 hours. Chill, uncovered, overnight. Makes 18 slices.

Peachy Diet Cheesecake

You can use the stenciled chocolate topping on other cheesecakes throughout the book.

Vanilla Cookie Crust

| 1¼ cups | finely crushed vanilla wafers |
| 3 tablespoons | butter or margarine, melted |

In a small bowl stir together crushed wafers and melted butter or margarine till well combined. Press crumb mixture evenly onto the bottom of a greased 9-inch springform pan.

Peach Filling

16 ounces	light cream cheese
12 ounces	tofu, well drained
½ cup	granulated sugar replacement
¼ cup	peach schnapps
2 tablespoons	cornstarch
2 teaspoons	vanilla extract
1 teaspoon	finely shredded lemon peel
1 or 2 drops	orange food coloring (optional)
6	egg whites
½ cup	puréed peaches

In a large bowl combine cream cheese, tofu, sugar replacement, peach schnapps, cornstarch, vanilla extract, lemon peel, and if desired, orange food coloring. Beat with an electric mixer till smooth. Stir in egg whites and puréed peaches. Pour the cream cheese mixture over the crust.

Bake at 225° for 1 hour and 20 minutes or till the center no longer looks wet or shiny. Remove the cake from the oven and run a knife around the inside edge of the pan. Turn the oven off; return the cake to the oven for an additional 2 hours. Chill, uncovered, overnight.

Cocoa Topping

| ¼ cup | unsweetened cocoa powder |
| 1 tablespoon | sugar |

Stir together cocoa powder and sugar. Place a decorative stencil over cheesecake. Sift cocoa powder mixture over stencil. Carefully remove stencil. Makes 18 slices.

Banana Dream Cheesecake

Fresh puréed bananas give this dessert a decisive richness.

Vanilla Cookie Crust

| 11 | vanilla sandwich cream cookies, crushed |
| 3 tablespoons | butter or margarine, melted |

In a small bowl stir together crushed cookies and melted butter or margarine till well combined. Press crumb mixture evenly onto the bottom of a greased 9-inch springform pan.

Banana Dream Filling

16 ounces	light cream cheese
12 ounces	tofu, well drained
½ cup	granulated sugar replacement
⅓ cup	puréed banana (1 small banana)
¼ cup	banana schnapps
2 tablespoons	cornstarch
2 teaspoons	vanilla extract
6	egg whites

In a large bowl combine cream cheese, tofu, sugar replacement, puréed banana, banana schnapps, cornstarch, and vanilla extract. Beat with an electric mixer till smooth. Stir in egg whites. Pour the cream cheese mixture over the crust.

Bake at 225° for 1 hour and 20 minutes or till the center no longer looks wet or shiny. Remove the cake from the oven and run a knife around the inside edge of the pan. Turn the oven off; return the cake to the oven for an additional 2 hours. Chill, uncovered, overnight. Makes 18 slices.

Carefree Cocoa Cheesecake

Go ahead! This decadent-tasting cheesecake is surprisingly low in calories.

Chocolate Cookie Crust

11	milk chocolate sandwich cream cookies, crushed
3 tablespoons	butter or margarine, melted

In a small bowl stir together crushed cookies and melted butter or margarine till well combined. Press crumb mixture evenly onto the bottom of a greased 9-inch springform pan.

Cocoa Filling

16 ounces	light cream cheese
12 ounces	tofu, well drained
3/4 cup	granulated sugar replacement
1/3 cup	unsweetened cocoa powder
1/4 cup	light sour cream
2 tablespoons	cornstarch
2 teaspoons	vanilla extract
12	egg whites

In a large bowl combine cream cheese, tofu, sugar replacement, cocoa powder, sour cream, cornstarch, and vanilla extract. Beat with an electric mixer till smooth. Stir in egg whites. Pour the cream cheese mixture over the crust.

Bake at 225° for 1 hour and 20 minutes or till the center no longer looks wet or shiny. Remove the cake from the oven and run a knife around the inside edge of the pan. Turn the oven off; return the cake to the oven for an additional 2 hours. Chill, uncovered, overnight. Makes 18 slices.

Slender Cherry Cheesecake

If you can't find fresh cherries, use canned cherries and drain them well.

Vanilla Cookie Crust

11	vanilla sandwich cream cookies, crushed
3 tablespoons	butter or margarine, melted

In a small bowl stir together crushed cookies and melted butter or margarine till well combined. Press crumb mixture evenly onto the bottom of a greased 9-inch springform pan.

Cherry Filling

16 ounces	light cream cheese
12 ounces	tofu, well drained
1/2 cup	granulated sugar replacement
1/4 cup	cherry schnapps
2 tablespoons	cornstarch
2 teaspoons	vanilla extract
1 teaspoon	finely shredded lemon peel
6	egg whites
1/3 cup	chopped bing cherries

In a large bowl combine cream cheese, tofu, sugar replacement, cherry schnapps, cornstarch, vanilla extract, and lemon peel. Beat with an electric mixer till smooth. Stir in egg whites and cherries. Pour the cream cheese mixture over the crust.

Bake at 225° for 1 hour and 20 minutes or till the center no longer looks wet or shiny. Remove the cake from the oven and run a knife around the inside edge of the pan. Turn the oven off; return the cake to the oven for an additional 2 hours. Chill, uncovered, overnight. Makes 18 slices.

Caramel Coffee Cheesecake

Vanilla Cookie Crust

11	vanilla sandwich cream cookies, crushed
3 tablespoons	butter or margarine, melted

In a small bowl stir together crushed cookies and melted butter or margarine till well combined. Press crumb mixture evenly onto the bottom of a greased 9-inch springform pan.

Caramel Coffee Filling

2 teaspoons	instant coffee
2 teaspoons	hot water
16 ounces	light cream cheese
12 ounces	tofu, well drained
1/2 cup	brown sugar replacement
1/4 cup	coffee-flavored liqueur
2 tablespoons	cornstarch
2 teaspoons	vanilla extract
12	egg whites

Stir together instant coffee and hot water till coffee dissolves. In a large bowl combine coffee, cream cheese, tofu, sugar replacement, coffee-flavored liqueur, cornstarch, and vanilla extract. Beat with an electric mixer till smooth. Stir in egg whites. Pour the cream cheese mixture over the crust.

Bake at 225° for 1 hour and 20 minutes or till the center no longer looks wet or shiny. Remove the cake from the oven and run a knife around the inside edge of the pan. Turn the oven off; return the cake to the oven for an additional 2 hours. Chill, uncovered, overnight. Makes 18 slices.

Blueberry Patch Cheesecake

Serve this blue-studded cheesecake with warm strawberry preserves for a festive Fourth of July treat.

Vanilla Cookie Crust

11	vanilla sandwich cream cookies, crushed
3 tablespoons	butter or margarine, melted

In a small bowl stir together crushed cookies and melted butter or margarine till well combined. Press crumb mixture evenly onto the bottom of a greased 9-inch springform pan.

Blueberry Filling

16 ounces	light cream cheese
12 ounces	tofu, well drained
1/2 cup	granulated sugar replacement
1/4 cup	blueberry schnapps
2 tablespoons	cornstarch
2 teaspoons	vanilla extract
1 teaspoon	finely shredded lemon peel
6	egg whites
1/2 cup	fresh blueberries

In a large bowl combine cream cheese, tofu, sugar replacement, blueberry schnapps, cornstarch, vanilla extract, and lemon peel. Beat with an electric mixer till smooth. Stir in egg whites and blueberries. Pour the cream cheese mixture over the crust.

Bake at 225° for 1 hour and 20 minutes or till the center no longer looks wet or shiny. Remove the cake from the oven and run a knife around the inside edge of the pan. Turn the oven off; return the cake to the oven for an additional 2 hours. Chill, uncovered, overnight. Makes 18 slices.

Index

Photography Credits

Food styling and all photography by Christopher Weeks. Christopher Weeks is a food and advertising photographer based in Tulsa, Oklahoma.

Additional food styling by Nancy Cooper and Mark and Traci Burnham.

p. 7, Grasshopper Cheesecake
Fabric: S. Harris

p. 15, Irish Cream Cheesecake
Fabric: S. Harris

p. 23, Chocolate Candy Cheesecake
Tableware: Pottery Barn

p. 35, Chocolate Cheesecake
Fabric: S. Harris

p. 47, Chocolate Coconut Almond Cheesecake
Fabric: S. Harris

p. 61, Ambrosia Cheesecake
Fabric: S. Harris

p. 65, Banana Split Cheesecake
Tableware: Pier 1

p. 71, Pear Elegance
Fabric: S. Harris
Tableware: Pier 1

p. 75, Strawberry Cheesecake
Fabric: S. Harris

p. 91, Super New York-Style Cheesecake
Tableware: Pier 1

p. 93, Dutch Vanilla Cheesecake
Fabric: Pier 1
Tableware: Pottery Barn

p. 95, Individual Cheesecake
Fabric: S. Harris
Tableware: Pottery Barn

p. 97, Very Vanilla Cheesecake
Fabric: S. Harris
Tableware: Pier 1

p. 107, Peachy Diet Cheesecake
Fabric: S. Harris
Tableware: Santa Fe Connection (Tulsa)

p. 4, Ingredients
Accessories: Mecca Gourmet

p. xii, Utensils
Accessories: Mecca Gourmet